Towards
an
Ecopsychotherapy

Mary-Jayne Rust

Towards
an
Ecopsychotherapy

Published in 2020 by Confer Books, London

www.confer.uk.com

Registered office:
21 California, Martlesham, Woodbridge, Suffolk IP12 4DE, England

3 5 7 9 10 8 6 4

This is a work of nonfiction. Any similarity between the characters and situations within its pages, and places, persons, or animals living or dead, could be unintentional and co-incidental. Some names and identifying details have been changed or omitted to, in part, protect the privacy of individuals.

British Library Cataloguing in Publication Data. A catalogue record for this book is available from the British Library.

ISBN: 978-1-913494-12-4 (paperback)
ISBN: 978-1-913494-13-1 (ebook)

Typeset by Bespoke Publishing Ltd.
Printed in the UK by Ashford Colour Press.

Contents

ACKNOWLEDGEMENTS

Great Gratitude to the Earth and all the creatures with whom we share this beautiful home, who suffer so much at the hands of humans.

Thanks to friends and colleagues who offered comments on early drafts of this book: Adrian Henriques, Dave Key, Emma Palmer, Hilary Prentice, Jane Ryan, Nick Totton.

INTRODUCTION

Ecopsychotherapy is a relatively new form of psycho-therapy which understands that human relationships exist within the larger context of life on earth. The web of life is not just a collection of beings but more like a continuum of earth–water–sky–tree–air–creatures–sun–human. Trauma arises when relation-ships within that continuum are disrupted; healing ourselves cannot be done in isolation. Psychotherapy invites us to tell the story of our human relationships; ecopsychotherapy expands this to include our earth story, the context or continuum in which our human relationships sit.

Ecopsychotherapy is just one of many ecother-apies which arise out of the field of ecopsychology, the inquiry into our human relationship with the rest of nature. Ecopsychotherapy is a form of ecotherapy which also pays attention to the inner world as well as to the therapist–client relationship. Being aware of power hierarchies within the therapy world I want to stress that this does not make ecopsychotherapy bet-ter than other forms of ecotherapy but simply offers a different approach that certain clients may benefit from. My chosen title *Towards an Ecopsychotherapy* speaks to this as an emergent field.

As climate chaos quickens and increasing numbers of people are waking up to the seriousness of our environmental crisis, we are becoming more aware of our dysfunctional relationship with the earth – the body on whom we depend for everything. This awakening to our crisis is double-edged. On the one hand it is very painful to witness the suffering of land, creatures, and peoples as a consequence of the system we inevitably take part in. On the other hand, the crisis is pushing us to remember we are part of the web of life in all its incredible richness and mystery. We are in relationship with the earth from the moment we are conceived in our mothers' watery wombs. We are all born into land, with its own particular qualities and atmospheres. We often speak of falling in love with a special place on this earth and feel bereft when this place is destroyed by so-called "development". Wandering outside to see a wide expanse of stars, or spending time in the mountains or by the sea, can be potent, transformative, and healing.

Many of us form important bonds with animals or trees. Our first experience of death in childhood might well be the loss of a beloved dog or cat. Some people escape from their dysfunctional families by seeking solace in the company of trees or with a close animal companion. A number of my clients may not have survived without these relationships; sometimes this has been their only experience in life of unconditional love. Gardens, parks, or beaches can be places of play where the doors to enchantment are opened. That is, of course, if we are privileged enough to have access to playing outdoors in childhood; for many, this has been replaced with play on screens, and those in urban areas may not have access to green space.

Yet most forms of psychotherapy and counselling focus on human relationships only. As early as 1960, psychoanalyst Harold Searles described how, "The nonhuman environment . . . is . . . considered as irrelevant to human personality development, and to the development of psychiatric illness . . . as though the human race were alone in the universe, pursuing individual and collective destinies in a homogenous matrix of nothingness" (1960, p. 3). This is part of a wider cultural attitude where we imagine we are separate from, and superior to, all other life forms. It is this context in which we are practising psychotherapy today. Naturally we are seeing a rise in what many call "eco-anxiety" or "eco-grief" as the situation worsens. These are not pathological symptoms to be treated by therapy; rather, they are healthy responses to a world in crisis which need to be shared and held in community.

Earth lawyer Polly Higgins named the extensive destruction of ecosystems "ecocide" and urged the Rome Statute of the International Criminal Court to recognise ecocide as the 5th Crime against Peace. As psychoanalyst Sally Weintrobe notes, "In framing ecocide as a war crime this bursts the gargantuan bubble of complacency that allows us to maintain the fiction that we are living in a time of peace" (Weintrobe, 2013, p. 1). Yet we continue.

The experience of psychotherapy tells us that change is neither easy nor linear. One part of the self wants to change while the other part wants to turn a blind eye, to carry on "as normal". Many feel relieved that large numbers of people have taken to the streets, as part of Extinction Rebellion and youth climate strikes, but others have complained of the "disruption" to their "normal" lives. A serious diagnosis does disrupt our daily routines! It requires us to step back and take a long hard look at where we are, in order to understand the roots of our malaise and how to bring ourselves back into balance.

This short book gives a flavour of ecopsychotherapy in practice, as well as its history, key themes, ideas, and controversies. Chapter 1 describes the practice of ecopsychotherapy outdoors. Chapter 2 takes a brief look at the history of ecotherapy as well as some of the diverse practices offered today, including the challenges facing this field. Chapter 3 offers an overview of ecopsychology giving some context and narrative for ecopsychotherapy. Chapters 4 and 5 return to the traditional setting of the therapy room, to explore the many ways in which our relationships with the more-than-human world enter into sessions. Chapter 4 focuses on how clients speak (or don't speak) about ecological crisis and how the therapist might respond. Chapter 5 explores how anthropocentrism comes into the work of therapy. Chapter 6 draws together some of the key threads of ecopsychotherapy. Chapter 7 goes beyond the very private practice of psychotherapy to look at the ways in which psychotherapeutic skills and insights might be of help to our dominant culture as we stumble towards an ecological civilisation, when many people are asking where we find hope during these troubled times. These chapters can be read in any order. For those who prefer to start with a theoretical overview, start with Chapter 3. For those wishing to start with ecopsychotherapy in the more traditional setting of the therapy room, start with Chapters 4 and 5. For those, like myself, who prefer to start with personal stories fresh from the woods, read the book as it is. Starting with practice, then finding a way to make sense of it, is how I learn. I have found this to be at odds with our dominant culture which often starts with concept before moving into practice.

All clinical material has permission to be shared and is heavily disguised.

A note about the word "nature": in order to avoid the way in which our language gives the impression that humans are separate from nature (e.g., "going out into nature") I will be using a range of phrases such as "other-than-human world", "more-than-human world", or "the rest of nature". I will sometimes capitalise Nature to mean the greater whole, the sacred web of life in whom we dwell.

Practising therapy outdoors

As I cross the threshold from tarmac to forest my senses are awakened: verdant green life abounds, the air is filled with bird conversations, with the rustling of trees, with the smell of leaves. I have space to breathe again. Views through the trees to the green hills beyond relax my perspective; what concerns might have been occupying my mind begin to fall away as I sink into my body. The rational mind, and its constant whirring of thoughts, gradually quietens. As the trees and I exchange our breath, I begin to see there is no sharp dividing line between my skin-encapsulated "self" and the rest of nature. The small "I" is now becoming aware of the larger self. Coming into relationship with the earth is literally grounding and has the capacity to stabilise the emotions and the whole body–mind. No wonder, then, that some therapists are working with clients outdoors.

In this chapter I will offer some of my own experiences of taking therapy outdoors and reflect on what this might offer to the process of individual psychotherapy. I started working outdoors with clients in 2007. At this point I had been immersed in the field of ecopsychology for a decade, during which time I had co-facilitated wilderness retreats on the west coast of Scotland with outdoor educator Dave Key. This experience confirmed for me that working with groups and individuals in wild places can be emotionally and spiritually transformative, in our relationship with our bodies and in our connection with the other-than-human world.

As I was considering how to offer therapy sessions outdoors my client Tina (who knew of my work as an ecopsychologist) asked if we could meet in the forest behind my house. We discussed this for some weeks, wondering together what this might mean to our work of several years. It felt like a huge leap into the unknown.

I had already been working as a therapist for over thirty years and, like most therapists, I had been trained to think of the therapy room as an important container for therapeutic work. The room remains unchanged from one month to the next and provides a safe, sealed environment for highly confidential, highly charged, sensitive and intimate exchanges. There were no trainings or guidance for working outdoors as a psychotherapist, although some therapists quietly admit to working in their gardens in the summer months.

Eventually Tina and I decided to meet at the edge of the forest, beside my house, at our usual session time. I invited her to lead the way through the woods where she found a sheltered spot to settle in, at the foot of a great oak. There was some awkwardness to begin with; the familiar chairs were gone and we were now on neutral ground, sitting side by side, shifting the power balance between us. As we settled into this place, feeling the warm shafts of sunlight filtering through the leaves, I noticed how deeply nourished and supported I felt as a therapist. The great oak who held our backs, providing a dazzling green canopy above, was part of the larger, living web containing us. While the relationship between the two of us remained central, the community of trees around us and all our relations who inhabit the forest (including dogs walking their humans) were now present in the session.

I also noticed that it took a little while to shake off a sense of unease, paranoia even, that I would be spotted by a colleague and "struck off" for transgression of boundaries! I gained confidence as I realised that this was a new form of therapeutic encounter which has become known as ecotherapy.

To begin with we continued with the same dialogue that we had been having indoors. But as the weeks passed we began to have some interesting meetings with others in the forest. I remember a moving moment in a session when Tina was unable to speak for some time. It was an anxious silence as I could tell she was feeling cut off and distressed; I tried to build a bridge with words, but the gap between us remained. This had happened in therapy sessions indoors many times previously. Tina's mother had been a perfectionist living in an abstract world of academia; in the transference I became her critical mother. In turn, she became the not-good-enough daughter, feeling that anything she said was stupid or meaningless. She might sometimes stay in this frozen state, unable to speak for long periods of the session.

As we sat together in the forest the silence between us was eased by the conversations of birds and the wind in the leaves. As I tried, again, to reach out to Tina I noticed that two squirrels were chasing each other around the tree trunk opposite us. I asked her if she felt chased by me; she smiled in acknowledgement. We fell into another silence. Then, at the same moment, we both glanced down to see the tiniest of spiders weaving a web between our shoulders. We grinned at each other, speechless with wonder at how the spider had built the bridge between us, making a deep connection without the need for words. We both sat back into a very different kind of silence: contemplative, awestruck. Knowing it was soon time to finish, Tina asked, "How are we going to get up now?" A good question to which I didn't have an answer. However, when we both glanced down again, the spider and her web had simply and completely vanished. In subsequent sessions we spoke of how the spider's web was an affirmation in trusting the connecting processes of life. Perhaps it also helped that we sat alongside each other against a tree, rather than in my room, which might have eased her feeling that I was "all powerful" over her.

Later that year Tina lost her mother. After some months of mourning her loss she announced in the middle of a session, "There is no new life." At that very moment an acorn dropped into her lap. The following spring, when she expressed a similar feeling of the impossibility of finding renewal, we both noticed a host of tiny caterpillars suspended on invisible threads, as if in mid-air, being gently blown by the breeze. These life-affirming responses to Tina's loss helped her in her state of mourning; in many ways the messages of life and death in the seasons' great round were saying things in a more straightforward way than I could.

SOME REFLECTIONS ON THE PROCESS

Taking psychotherapy into the forest offers a different and creative way of working. Unlike the room, the outdoors is constantly changing and speaks to the inner process, and interpersonal dynamics, if we know how to listen. The natural language of the other-than-human world offers metaphors and mirrors which enable us to step back and see ourselves from another perspective, moving us from rational to imaginative, from linear to storytelling. There is a sense of expanded awareness as we come into an experience of what ecopsychologists call the ecological self (a concept outlined in Chapter 3).

Tina's story shows how the power relationship between therapist and client can be changed through therapist and client entering a shared space, with no routine sitting places. This, in turn, eased a dynamic in the transference that tended to become frozen indoors. Other writers have made similar observations (Jordan, 2005, p. 50).

Some writers have introduced the idea that working outdoors moves the therapy dyad to a triangle: therapist – client – nature. There is now a "third" present in the session (Jordan, 2005, p. 50; Brazier, 2018, pp. 79–93). This idea has been used within art therapy, to suggest a triangulation between therapist, client, and image. Others suggest that nature becomes a co-therapist or a therapeutic partner (Jordan, 2005, p. 121; Berger, 2006). This holds when we think of a tree as the third, for example. But when we extend "the third" to Nature as the greater living whole in whom we dwell, this becomes more confusing since we are in Nature all the time, whether indoors or outdoors. In this way the terms "'third" or "co-therapist" seem to me to be rather lacking to describe something as ineffable as Nature.

TRANSRATIONAL EXPERIENCES

Synchronicities happen in abundance outdoors; other practitioners also remark on this (Totton, 2011, p. 160). Jung defines synchronicity as two things coming together in time, simultaneously, which are connected through meaning, not through cause and effect (Jung, 1955). Such moments offer a portal into another way of seeing the world where we have an experience that everything and everyone is in continuous dynamic relationship within a unified reality from which everything emerges and to which everything returns. Jung and Pauli referred to this matrix as *unus mundus*, Latin for "one world". In this way, synchronicity is like an intervention of grace offering an experience of wholeness (Main, 2007).

Jung believed that synchronicity serves a role similar to that of dreams; the spider's web, for example, offered Tina and me an image which spoke to the unconscious. Jung describes an occasion when a female patient, who was caught in a highly polished Cartesian rationalism, brings a dream in which someone had given her a golden scarab.

> *While she was still telling me this dream, I heard something behind me gently tapping on the window . . . I opened the window . . . and caught the insect in the air as it flew in. It was a scarabaeid beetle, whose green-gold colour nearly resembles that of a gold scarab. I handed the beetle to my patient with the words, "Here is your scarab." . . . This experience punctured the desired hole in her rationalism and broke the ice of her intellectual resistance. The treatment could now be continued with satisfactory results. (Jung, 1955, pp. 525–526)*

The beetle, symbolic of rebirth in some cultures, is able to penetrate her defence and bring her into another way of seeing the world.

The idea of synchronicity is hardly new; Indigenous cultures worldwide respect synchronicity and use it for guidance. Synchronous events have the potential to dramatically shift perspective in worldviews – from the Western view that the dream emerges from the personal psyche, to a view that we are immersed in a collective dream where synchronicity is there all the time if we are able to notice.

Sometimes a particular smell appears while working in the woods. On one occasion my client, Anne, was telling me about her childhood and the multiple losses she had experienced. At the centre of this was the loss of her mother at a very young age; she found it very painful that she had so few memories of her mother. Suddenly we both noticed a strong smell of perfume in the air and yet no one was, or had been, anywhere near us. We were both baffled. After a while my client wondered if this scent was "a presence"; when she made the link to her mother, the smell disappeared. On another occasion my client, Eleanor, described how a wind with a scent of rose had blown into her face at a moment of profound insight about coming into the present moment as a way of healing loss. This is known as "clairsalience" or "clairscent", one of the many intuitive ways of perceiving the world beyond our five senses. From my experience it seems that being outdoors, in the woods, seems to support a more intuitive knowing as these occurrences have not (yet) happened indoors.

EMBODIMENT, INTUITION, AND CHOICE OF SPOT

Being outdoors encourages a sinking down into the body, a relaxation and rebalancing of the body–mind which enables presence in the moment. The senses are awakened: there are multiple smells, sounds of birdsong, and quite possibly some beautiful sights.

As we wander through the woods I invite my client to lead; this can enable a more embodied approach to choosing the path or which spot to settle in. Do the feet lead, is there a gut or heart decision, or perhaps it is possible to follow a smell like a dog? Or perhaps there is a "sign" from the more-than-human world which affirms the "right" place? For some a place just "feels" right intuitively; for others this decision-making process can be quite anxiety-provoking, especially if she or he is unable to access an embodied way of being.

Sometimes a choice of spot is made quite unconsciously. One client settled on a bench where five paths crossed at a time when he was making some important decisions between different paths in life. When my client Eleanor lost her sister, in very tragic circumstances, she wanted to return to working outdoors, explaining to me that she felt closer to her outside. The spot she chose for us to meet was on the trunk of a great fallen oak tree, the branches providing a semi-hidden place; yet it took some time to see the significance of this place.

ECO-GRIEF IN THE FOREST

Litter in urban woodland is just one manifestation of the shadow of consumer culture, a reminder of our lack of care for the earth. One day, my client, Rachel, assembled a range of plastic items found on the forest floor. She broke down and wept as she told me, "There is no wild place left on the planet that is untouched by human greed and lack of care. I try my best to care but everything I use and buy is part of this destructive system and it's just getting worse. I can't bear it anymore. Sometimes I think it would be much better if humans were just wiped out." As we sat together under the strength of the oak, exploring more of Rachel's despair, grief, and anger, a blackbird perched on a black plastic bag amid her artwork and sang with the clearest of notes. In this poignant moment Rachel saw that beauty and destructiveness are intrinsic to everything and everyone in Nature, including humans, including herself. This recognition allowed her to move out of a place of wanting all humans to be gone and into a place of wanting to defend the web of life, in which we have our rightful place. Eventually she found her niche in taking creative action; there she found a different kind of hope which is more about living in the present and in relationship.

While the therapy room holds great consistency, which might be just what some clients need at times, the outdoors offers a changing scene in which the polarities of life – such as the great round of life and death, or light and dark, despair and hope – are held together. I will return to eco-grief in Chapter 4.

THE FRAME: BOUNDARIES AND PRACTICALITIES

Taking psychotherapy outdoors raises many questions. For this reason, when a client comes to me for ecotherapy, I invite her or him for an initial session indoors in order to talk through some of the benefits and challenges posed by working outdoors. The client might ask: what if we meet someone that one of us knows? What if someone interrupts us during the session? In my experience these situations rarely occur and can easily be dealt with when they do.

Assessment: The first session also gives me the chance to assess whether I think working outdoors is right for this client at this time. For example, loud emoting is best done indoors as this will alarm others in the vicinity. There may also be some states of mind which need the tight containment of a room. In *Naturecure*, Richard Mabey writes movingly about how he chose to face the wall, rather than the window overlooking his garden, after his breakdown. He was severely depressed at the time and describes how he felt let down by the other-than-human world, which had previously been a place of such joy and nourishment for him (Mabey, 2007).

Confidentiality: Concerns about confidentiality and safety are obviously fundamental, especially when working in an urban forest or park which is open to the public. It is for this reason that I suggest we find a spot to settle in that is away from the path; some clients choose a more hidden spot. While some therapists offer "walk and talk therapy" I find this does not work in my location because the paths through the woods are often single file and there are times when we are passing others with the risk of being overheard.

Threshold and reciprocity: For the first session outdoors I arrange to meet my client at a spot on the edge of the woods. We create an imaginary threshold and ask permission of the forest community (out loud or silently) to enter for our work together. This reminds us the woods are not a "resource" that we are "using" for ourselves; rather, this signals that we are entering a sacred space or temenos where we are in reciprocal relationship with the other-than-human world at all times. Every being whom we encounter holds meaning, in the same way that all elements of a dream hold meaning. Indoor therapy also has some ritual elements: the client rings the bell and steps over the threshold of the building and into the temenos of the therapy room, although usually this is not made explicit.

At the end of the session we return to the threshold and offer thanks for whatever seems relevant that day. We might also think together about what we give back to the earth in return for her immense generosity:

picking up litter is one possibility, making a physical offering is another.

Familiarity with the land: It is essential for the therapist to have some relationship with the land before offering therapy sessions there. Each tree, each plant, each animal offers different qualities to the session if we know how to listen; the land itself may hold a range of different histories. It is wise to know if there have been any traumatic events in the past, such as land clearances or plague burials, as some clients may feel what the land may be holding. In countries where Indigenous peoples have been displaced by white settlers it is wise for ecotherapists to know something of the peoples whose land they are on and to be aware of whether they need permission to be in this place.

Flexibility – outdoors and indoors: Some clients prefer a mix of working indoors and outdoors, depending on weather, needs, and mood. This can lead to some interesting enquiry into the intention behind the choice of location.

There has been a tendency within the world of ecopsychology to assume that all ecotherapy practice takes place outdoors. I would agree with other practitioners who suggest that ecotherapy practice can also take place indoors (Doherty, 2016, pp. 30–31). I do not feel that outdoors is always better, but it does bring our relationship with the other-than-human world into the present: the sky can be felt, the earth can be touched. There may also be occasions when a client has experienced trauma in a room (sexual abuse or torture, for example) and the experience of "enclosure" is too difficult to bear. For others the protection of the room is vital. Experience of ecopsychotherapy has taught me that the room is both a protection from outside intrusions as well as a barrier to nourishment and useful information from Nature in both a literal and transpersonal sense.

SUMMARY

Spending time immersed in the more-than-human world can change the way we think and feel; in turn, this changes our relationships with both inner and outer nature. Working as a therapist outdoors can change the therapy relationship as well as the practice of psychotherapy itself.

The benefits of working therapeutically outdoors are many and varied, going beyond what I have been able to cover in this chapter. These might include: the more-than-human world as a non-judgemental space in which the voice of the inner critic can be softened for a while; the wonder, awe, and beauty of the forest, mountains, or sea can offer a portal to an experience of deep mystery and timelessness; cold, rain, or the shadows of the forest can offer a gateway into exploring fears and anxieties; a sense of Nature as origin – both in this life as well as in the life of our species; relationship between place and childhood memories; explorations of adventure and risk; the creativity of the more-than-human world offers a space for relaxation, play, and free association stirring the imagination.

$$\textbf{2}$$

The diverse range of ecotherapy practices

In this chapter I will look at some of the early roots of ecotherapy as well as a selection of ecotherapy practices which have developed since the 1960s. I will also consider some of the challenges within this field such as the difficulty of taking ecotherapy into mainstream culture and the ongoing issue of cultural appropriation.

Humans have always sought inspiration, healing, and vision in wild nature, away from human community. Aboriginal peoples go on walkabout; Native Americans fast on vision quests; the Celts went on pilgrimages in the hills; yogis, sages, poets, and artists know that immersion in the wilderness offers us the possibility of radical transformation of consciousness.

Making such a journey can involve great risk. Malidoma Somé, an African shaman of the Dagara people, describes how some of the young men who go into the wilds for a ritual initiation into adulthood do not return (Somé, 1995). This might seem shocking to our society, so obsessed with health and safety. Yet, as wilderness guide Bill Plotkin points out, "[T]he small risk of death is preferable to the living death of an uninitiated life. Besides, when we compare Dagara society to our own, we find an even greater percentage of teenagers die – through suicide, substance abuse and gang warfare – in their unsuccessful attempts to initiate themselves" (Plotkin, 2003, p. 37). Those who survive their time in the wilds will have been offered a multitude of teachings from wild nature. Wilderness is not only a place which soothes the human soul; an immersion in wilderness offers an awe-inspiring experience full of dangers which can strip away the ego, offering a form of psychic death, enabling a deeper connection with the greater whole, the Great Mystery. In this respect, Nature is our greatest shrink.

However, as humans increasingly domesticate the earth – and for the most part we are now the top predator – it becomes increasingly difficult to have an experience of being in the presence of something more powerful than ourselves. In the UK, for example, the land has become so tamed that time in Nature can become a one-dimensional "beautiful" experience, lacking the grit that enables us to grow and learn from the powerful "other". In this sense, climate change and the ecological crisis are like an act of Nature rising up, showing humans who is in charge, offering our dominant culture an opportunity for a collective rite of passage. Facing our own extinction could be seen as the Mother of all Rites of Passage for Western civilisation.

THE EARLY ROOTS OF ECOTHERAPY

A number of modern forms of wilderness practice started to arise in the late 1960s, such as the School of Lost Borders, in California, which offers wilderness rites of passage experiences to young people and adults (Foster & Little, 1989) and the Animas Valley Institute, in Colorado (Plotkin, 2003). From 1969 Robert Greenway offered wilderness group experiences for many summers, lasting from two to four weeks; this began with his psychology students and expanded to include the entire community at Sonoma State University,

California. Everything short of life-threatening situations was decided by consensus within the group. Participants had life-changing experiences which Greenway describes as "the wilderness effect", a combination of cleaning out the poisons of our culture; a sense of expansion of self; reconnection with our ancient past and deeper psyches; release of repression. However, Greenway points out how hard it is to find adequate language to describe these experiences because at its core is a meeting with something "ineffable" or "spiritual". He also came to realise how difficult it was for some people to integrate their experiences on their return home. In some cases this could lead to severe depression, described more recently by ecotherapist Martin Jordan (2005). Therefore careful preparation and post-experience support needs to be put in place for the "wilderness effect" to be reintegrated into everyday life (Greenway, 1995, p. 122).

Usiko is a South African organisation for young people at risk, based on Indigenous rites-of-passage practices in wilderness combined with modern therapeutic interventions. Usiko works with adolescents from townships, gang communities, and remote rural settlements who are often involved in violence resulting in imprisonment. The organisation draws on elders from the community as mentors as well as those experienced in therapeutic wilderness practice. Storytelling is central to their process (http://usiko.org.za/; Pinnock & Douglas Hamilton, 1997).

These are just two examples of many more initiatives which are marrying ancient and modern practices.

CLOSER TO HOME

A great many outdoor therapeutic practices have arisen since the 1960s such as horticultural therapy, environmental arts therapies, adventure therapy, nature therapy, and animal-facilitated therapy. These diverse practices come under the umbrella term of ecotherapy, the practice of ecopsychology. Ecopsychotherapy is a more recent development.

There has been a variety of research to show how spending time outdoors – in the garden or local park, walking by the sea or in the mountains – can have a beneficial effect on human health, both physical and psychological (for a summary of research see e.g., Jordan, 2014, ch. 1). Patients in hospital, for example, heal more quickly when they have access to a garden; even a window with a green view speeds up recovery time (Cooper Marcus & Barnes, 1998). Many of us know that being in the presence of the beauty of nature is healing for the soul. Some of us will know how things can fall into place on a long walk: a dilemma troubling the mind at the start seems to have effortlessly resolved itself by the end. In 2007 the mental health charity MIND (UK) produced a report to show that spending time outdoors can help anxiety, mild to moderate depression, and a range of other difficulties, due to a combination of factors such as reducing stress levels, relaxing the body–mind, affect regulation, as well as spending time in natural light (MIND, 2007).

Neurologist Oliver Sacks writes:

> *In many cases, gardens and nature are more powerful than any medication . . . My friend Lowell has moderately severe Tourette's syndrome. In his usual busy, city environment, he has hundreds of tics and verbal ejaculations each day – grunting, jumping, touching things compulsively. I was therefore amazed one day when we were hiking in a desert to realize that his*

*tics had completely disappeared. The re-
moteness and uncrowdedness of the scene,
combined with some ineffable calming
effect of nature, served to defuse his ticcing,
to "normalize" his neurological state, at
least for a time. (as quoted in Rubin, 2019)*

It is no surprise, then, at this point of history,
when humans within industrial growth culture are
probably at the peak of dissociation, that therapists
are experimenting with working outdoors in diverse
ways, with different rationales and practices. Below
are some examples; many of the projects described
are familiar to me and are located in the UK.

RELATIONSHIPS WITH PLANTS

Indigenous peoples have a long tradition of consulting
and revering plants as teachers. Their use of plants as
medicines comes from communicating with plants
rather than using trial and error or analytical research
(Buhner, 2004, p. 2). There is a growing plant consciousness community who are exploring healing
with the conscious intelligence of plants; they draw

on ancient knowledge of relationships and communication with plants, including shamanic knowledge (https://plantconsciousness.com/; Buhner, 2004).

The use of horticulture to calm the senses can be traced as far back as 2000 BC in ancient Mesopotamia (Detweiler et al., 2012). There has been a long tradition of horticulture therapy in the UK, in institutions such as prisons and mental hospitals. Simply spending time in the garden, tilling the soil and tending to the growing plants, is therapeutic.

When psychotherapist Jenny Grut set up The Natural Growth Project in 1992 she began a new tradition of taking psychotherapy onto the land. Grut valued both the therapeutic experience of spending time on the land and an awareness of the inner world, creating a new form of ecopsychotherapy. This project was part of the Medical Foundation for Victims of Torture, based on allotments (community gardens) in North London.

Grut was a psychotherapist from Chile, working with asylum seekers and refugees. She recognised these clients had difficulty in talking about their problems in small cramped rooms, some of them associating such spaces with a traumatic past. Many clients brought strong memories of gardens, fields, or farms back home with affection or joy. Grut therefore felt that this client group needed to start by making a relationship with the land because their relationships with other humans had been so profoundly broken. She used the potent metaphors of gardening in the therapy dialogue but emphasised this has to be done with care. "For obvious reasons, 'deadheading' is an expression to be avoided, whereas weeding can be a way of sorting out thoughts and relationships – 'weeds of the mind' . . . Watering, if excessive, may indicate over-caring, smothering, being fearful, or an emotional leakage . . . The unconscious message from the client might read: 'Can the plants survive on very little, as I did?'" (Linden & Grut, 2002, pp. 42–43). Grut also remarked to me how she could walk past the various plots at the end of the day and see something of each person's inner world reflected in the state of their plot. The Natural Growth Project offered another very important dimension: people could gather as a multicultural community and feast together on their home-grown vegetables, thus providing far more than individual therapy. Many other similar projects have since taken root in different parts of the UK.

RELATIONSHIPS WITH TREES

According to Buddhist texts, Buddha attained enlightenment by meditating for forty-nine days under a sacred fig tree, known by its heart-shaped leaves. Forests have long been a place of sanctuary for many forms of life including humans. "Dod yn ôl at fy nghoed" is a Welsh phrase which means "to return to a balanced state of mind", but literally means "to return to my trees". Most of us within Western culture have lost our capacity to listen to, and communicate with, trees. Yet this ancient capacity survives in a few people and it seems that, increasingly, many people are able to retrieve it with practice, as if exercising a withered muscle.

Ian Siddons Heginworth has developed the practice of environmental arts therapy in relation to trees and the Celtic cycle of the year. Each tree offers different qualities and metaphors to the inner work of therapy, which can be "felt into" at particular times of the year. He writes,

> *The silver birch is often the first tree to colonise a wood and the first to leaf in spring, so it is about new beginnings . . . The Hazel*

tree was associated with wisdom, intuition and creativity; Hazel rods were used for divining water and minerals, and so it helps to attune us to the deep undercurrents within the earth and within ourselves . . . Elders are hunched, twisted and wizened trees and were often associated with witches . . . the elder personifies the crone, the feminine as elder . . . Each month has offered us the Tree of life in a different guise, twelve different faces of wisdom shaped by the season into metaphors that are meaningful to us then and only then . . . feel our way into any one of these in their rightful time and the depth of the lesson can be profound and transformative for this is a teaching of the heart so the mind can only truly understand it when it has been felt in context with the turning year. (Siddons Heginworth, 2008, pp. 23, 130, 173, 178)

RELATIONSHIPS WITH ANIMALS

Animal-assisted therapy has early roots also: Freud noticed his dog Jo-Fi would pick up moods of patients, as well as helping them to relax in sessions, particularly children and adolescents (Coren & Walker, 1997, p. 78). *The Horse Boy* tells a moving story of Rowan, a four-year-old boy diagnosed with autism, who does not speak, suffers from frequent raging fits, and is often distant and hostile. His father, Rupert Isaacson, describes a remarkable meeting between Rowan and a local horse, Betsy, who stood stock-still and bowed her head, wide-eyed and quivering. When lifted onto her back, Rowan was immediately calmed and started to speak. Over the years Rowan has been transformed through equine assisted therapy, although Isaacson takes care to say that he is "healed not cured". He also describes how part of his healing is due to the movement when riding the horse, and the effect this has on the brain (Isaacson, 2009). The Isaacson family has set up The Horse Boy Foundation to make equine therapy and kinetic learning available to help other children.

Psychotherapist Kelvin Hall is a practitioner of equine assisted therapy; he refers to the retrieval of our previously buried capacity to communicate with animals as "remembering the forgotten tongue", and that when "the yearning for connection [with the other-than-human world] is met the hunger to consume is less" (Hall, 2012a, p. 79). Here he describes the results of bringing horses into relationship with clients in therapy:

> *Explorers in this field have discovered that the range of messages and responses horses offer is vast. The degree to which they can immediately reflect and respond to human mood, attitude – and changes in these – is awesome and very sensitive. They often show the human their unowned anger, fear, sorrow or resentment. When the human reclaims these feelings, allows them and moves beyond them, the horse offers calm and co-operation. When humans whose boundaries have been violated, learn to assert their boundaries, horses show respect and acceptance. They reward clear intention, respect and enthusiasm with agility, grace and power. (Hall, 2012b)*

Animals can also come into the therapy relationship in more symbolic ways. In her paper reflecting on our relationships with dogs and inner landscapes Jungian analyst Julia Ryde describes how her client finds meaning in some accidental encounters with Ryde's dog:

> *When my dog came into my life, I found dogs began to creep into the material I was listening to in different ways, both directly and indirectly. A patient said she saw me in the park trying to control my "wild" dog – obviously from her tone of voice not very well. My "wild" dog was a puppy at the time and we were still getting to know each other. She also encountered my dog one day trying to get to us through the connecting door, which separates my consulting room from the rest of the house. Her feelings of identification with the dog, we discovered . . . were to do with: feeling trapped in my house/mother's body; a wild/instinctual part of her which is not allowed in my consulting room; but also*

*the younger sibling brother born after her
who is being left outside of the consulting
room just as she felt she was left out when
he was born. (Ryde, 2010, p. 481)*

ELEMENTAL RELATIONSHIPS

Relationships with animals and plants are familiar to many people who live with animal companions or who tend their gardens. It is not uncommon to hear of people speaking of elemental relationships with stone, air, fire, and water. During time spent co-facilitating week-long ecotherapy residentials on the west coast of Scotland, I have noticed how men often speak of being drawn to a relationship with stone, while women often speak of their relationship with water.

Carl Jung had a deep connection with stone which reminded him of his age-old self; he wrote:

*At such times [of conflict and brooding on
God, etc.] it was strangely reassuring and
calming to sit on my stone. Somehow it
would free me of all my doubts. Whenever
I thought that I was the stone, the conflict*

> ceased. "The stone has no uncertainties, no
> urge to communicate, and is eternally the
> same for thousands of years," I would think,
> "while I am only a passing phenomenon
> which bursts into all kinds of emotions, like
> a flame that flares up quickly and then goes
> out." I was but the sum of my emotions, and
> the "Other" in me was the timeless imper-
> ishable stone. (Jung, 1961, p. 59)

Later he describes how his wife's death "wrenched me violently out of myself. It cost me a great deal to regain my footing and contact with stone helped me" (1961, pp. 174–175).

Water holds a very different quality of flow and is often associated with emotional and intuitive intelligence, with the moon, and the unconscious. It is also seen as a mirror for the soul. Traditionally it is known for its purification qualities but it can also overwhelm and drown, relating to fears of boundlessness, letting go, and surrender.

Fire has a transformative power. In Greek mythology the phoenix, a bird associated with the sun, rises from the ashes of its predecessor symbolising renewal after death. As I write this text many forests of the world, some of them ancient rainforests, are on fire. At the same time, other parts of the world are flooded. Fire and water are two of the foundational elements of life. There are many ways to understand how these elements are reflected in the human psyche. I find myself flooded with watery grief in response to what is happening in the world, as well as ablaze with anger at the many injustices. By developing a relationship with fire and water it is possible to transmute the associated emotions.

WILD THERAPY

Wild therapy, developed by Nick Totton, explores the polarised themes of wildness and domestication which run throughout human history and culture; it supports the spontaneous and the unknown, trusting what arises of its own accord; it also recognises embodiment as a central aspect of our existence. It is explicit about reciprocity and stating that it enriches the therapy work as well as our relationship with the earth. Unlike most other ecotherapies, wild therapy offers a practice and theoretical understanding that is not dependent on working outdoors, "Wild therapy might not *look* very different from a lot of therapy that is already practised . . . it does not require – though it may well include – exotic techniques and direct involvement outdoors . . . It is an attitude of mind, rather than a bag of tricks" (Totton, 2011, p. 183). Further, Totton points out that mainstream psychotherapy and counselling have become too identified with domestication and associated concepts like boundaries, objectivity, and control; wild therapy seeks to rebalance the practice of therapy itself (Totton, 2011).

ECOTHERAPY: ISSUES, CHALLENGES, AND CONTROVERSIES

There are a number of interesting and challenging issues within the field of ecotherapy. One of the dangers is that ecotherapy is subsumed into mainstream culture only to become a panacea for the ills of Western culture through a familiar one-way taking from nature. The language and methods used can reflect this, such as offering "techniques" (sometimes borrowed from Indigenous traditions without permission) to privileged white people to "go out into nature" (at worst, flying or driving long distances to get there, with no experience of the land or its history) in order to "reconnect" and "get healed" based on the idea that if we can just "love nature" we will no longer harm "the environment". I am caricaturing an approach, here, in order to communicate an attitude within ecotherapy practice where there is little sense of relationship or *reciprocity* with the rest of nature and little awareness of cultural appropriation. While this is no doubt offered with the best of intentions, this version of ecotherapy is in danger of perpetuating the damage brought about by our Western worldview. Nature writer Richard Mabey cautions against a simplistic version of ecotherapy which suggests that all we have to do is go out on a sunny day and look at the pretty bluebell wood and everything will be OK. He continues, "This is not only insulting to the complexity of human beings but also deeply insulting to the complexity of nature" (Mabey, 2012).

We all know how difficult it is to live in relationship. Human relationships are fraught with conflict: the complexities of difference, love, hate, joy, grief, disappointment, judgement, power struggles, and more. Intimacy is where our most vulnerable selves are exposed. There are similar and different psychological dynamics at play within our relationship with the other-than-human world, especially when we have barely begun to disentangle the raft of projections we (as part of industrial growth culture) place on nature as "the other" (Rust, 2009, 2011). Addressing these complex dynamics is part of the work of ecopsychotherapy.

First-generation ecopsychologists (Roszak, Kanner, & Gomes, 1995) were very clear that our attempts to "reconnect" with the more-than-human world are deeply affected by the Western worldview that shapes the way we view "nature" as a set of objects to be used, rather than Nature as a sacred matrix, the living breathing web of life of whom we are a small part. In their view ecopsychology, and its practice, cannot avoid being a political field as it challenges the value systems, choices, and lifestyles of our dominant culture. It can therefore never be subsumed into mainstream culture without losing its very essence. Andy Fisher writes,

> "In a therapeutic-recollective sense, [ecopsy-
> chology] is about mending the split
> between psyche and nature through recall-
> ing the mind's deep rootedness in earthly
> relations. In a critical sense, it is about ad-

*dressing the social sources of violence done
to both human and more-than-human
nature, identifying the historical, cultural,
political, and economic roots of our ecopsy-
chological crisis" (2013, p. 167).*

Yet, as Fisher notes, there is a second generation of
ecopsychologists who are trying to align ecopsychology within mainstream psychology and, in the process,
causing it to lose some of its radical nature (ibid.).

CULTURAL APPROPRIATION

Since ecotherapy is a practice which is about remembering our relationship with the land, it is not
surprising that many practitioners seek inspiration
from Indigenous cultures who have sophisticated
earth-related practices and cosmologies which have
lasted for thousands of years. For example, Jeannette
Armstrong (quoted on pages 68-69 in this text) writes
from the Okanagan view, which offers the reader a
startlingly different perspective on self in relation to
the earth.

Yet there are, for obvious reasons, highly sensitive issues here. We all know of the atrocities of genocide and cultural genocide that Indigenous peoples worldwide have endured at the hands of white people. It is therefore quite understandable when Indigenous peoples feel it is the last straw when westerners, broken by the ills of their culture, now idealise and seek spiritual guidance from the very cultures which have been so abused by their white ancestors. Writer Pegi Eyers (2016) suggests that we must stop using terms and practices such as "vision quest" or "medicine walk", which originate from native cultures, and instead seek guidance from our own ancestry: white people of European ancestry can return to their own rich and diverse sources of European Indigenous Knowledge (EIK), such as Celtic animism, Norse cosmology, or the wisdom of *wyrd* in Anglo-Saxon cosmology (Bates, 1983).

My own experience has been to seek inspiration from a variety of freely offered sources. Here is a small selection: the writings of Indigenous peoples (e.g., Armstrong, 1995; Somé, 1995; Deloria, 2009; Prechtel, 2009; Wall Kimmerer, 2013); learning from westerners who have lived with Indigenous peoples for prolonged lengths of time and who have been building bridges between Indigenous and Western ways of knowing (e.g., Norberg-Hodge, 1992; Abram, 1997; Bernstein, 2005; Colin Campbell, personal communication; Annie Spencer, personal communication); learning from westerners who have been digging deep into our own ancestral ways (e.g., Bates, 1983; Baring & Cashford, 1991; Siddons Heginworth, 2008; Breytenbach, 2012; Blackie, 2016).

These writers, colleagues, and friends have given me invaluable insights into earth-related worldviews and the way of life that springs from them. Without these alternative visions I would have found it difficult to see outside the cultural box I was raised in when our language, lifestyles, and thinking are so steeped in these values. Notions such as: "people belong to the land, land does not belong to people" (UN Declaration on the Rights of Indigenous Peoples) or "the landscape is our second skin" (Power, 2012) or "the word for body literally means the land-dreaming capacity" (Armstrong, 1995, for full quote see p. 68 in this text) have the capacity to startle and help us to rethink our familiar ways of seeing. This has supported me in listening more deeply to the land and the other-than-human world, turning to my own intuition and bodily knowing to create practices to re-embed into the land and to reflect on the practice of ecopsychotherapy.

SUMMARY

There are many different forms of ecotherapy, which operate on different levels. Some ecotherapies draw solely on the benefits of spending time outdoors which are both physical and psychological. At the other end of the spectrum there are forms of ecotherapy, such as ecopsychotherapy, which pay attention to the relationship between inner and outer worlds as well as the transference between therapist and client and/or group dynamic. It is worth noting that being outdoors is not essential for ecopsychotherapy because it is more about a change in understanding self in relation to Nature than it is about a change in place. However, as I have tried to illustrate here, the experience of taking therapy outdoors can very much support this change in understanding. I will return to these ideas in Chapters 5 and 6 where I discuss ecopsychotherapy in the traditional setting of the therapy room.

Different forms of ecotherapies are suitable for different client groups. I am mindful of the power hierarchies that have developed within the therapy world and therefore wish to stress that there is no "right" way to practise. However, it is vital to pay attention to cultural appropriation as well as maintaining professional client–therapist boundaries. It is also apparent that a new form of working therapeutically is emerging out of the times we are living through; central to this is the notion of reciprocity, where healing the individual and healing the earth are indivisible.

3

Ecopsychology: context, frame, narrative

This chapter looks at the history and narrative of ecopsychology. I will point to some of the central concepts within this field of inquiry showing how these ideas offer a conceptual framework for the case material presented. The reader will see how the seeds of this field have been present in some of the earliest writings and practice of psychotherapy as well as in the thinking of the more relational ecologists.

Ecopsychology has arisen in the last few decades in response to industrial growth culture and its destructive effects on the earth; it began in the USA but also has roots in the UK and Europe, South Africa, Australia, New Zealand, and more recently in

Taiwan and Hong Kong. The word ecopsychology was first coined by Roszak (1992) although Greenway (1995) was using the term psych-ecology as early as the 1960s. Ecopsychology is most commonly defined as an inquiry into our human relationship with the rest of nature.

Ecopsychology is a divergent field, more like a complex web than a linear path; any overview is therefore selective and incomplete, with many different paths in and many close relations: deep ecology (Naess, 1973), human geography, transpersonal ecology (Fox, 1990; Maiteny, 2012), nature spirituality, and more. These overlapping fields are reaching for ways to reunite *ecos* and *psyche*, one of the many splits resulting from the Western analytic mindset. It can therefore be described as the study (*logos*) of the soul (*psyche*) in its natural home (*ecos*).

Ecopsychology draws on many lineages: Indigenous traditions and cosmology (e.g., Armstrong, 1995; Somé, 1995; Wall Kimmerer, 2013); Buddhist cosmology (e.g., Macy, 1990; Brazier, 2018); the long tradition of experience in the wilderness (e.g., Foster & Little, 1989; Greenway, 1995; Key, 2003, pp. 18–33); ecofeminism (e.g., Griffin, 1979; Merchant, 1983; LaChappelle,

1992; Plumwood, 1992); eco-philosophy (e.g., Abram, 1997); deep ecology (e.g., Sessions, 1995); Western psychology (e.g., DuNann Winter, 1996). Early leading ecological thinkers with a depth view include: Aldo Leopold (1949), who rejected a utilitarian, human-centred view of the land and called for a new "land ethic" dealing with humans' relationship to land, animals, and plants; Rachel Carson's seminal book *Silent Spring* (1962) brought attention to pesticide abuse and the human domination of nature, showing how human wellbeing depends on the wellbeing of the earth; Gregory Bateson (1972) wrote about an "ecology of mind" bringing systems thinking to the fore.

A central narrative of ecopsychology is that we once knew we were part of the web of life – physically, psychologically, and spiritually – and in the course of our long history we have become increasingly disconnected from the rest of nature. Roszak wrote,

> *Once upon a time all psychologies were "ecopsychologies". Those who sought to heal the soul took for granted that human nature is densely embedded in the world we share with animal, vegetable, mineral, and*

all the unseen powers of the cosmos . . . It
is the psychiatry of modern western society
that has split the "inner life" from the "out-
er world" – as if what was inside of us was
not also inside the universe, something real,
consequential, and inseparable from our
study of the natural world. (1992, p. 14)

C. G. Jung was the first psychotherapist to write extensively about the importance of our relationship with the earth and the consequences of our modern lifestyles; he wrote:

Through scientific understanding, our
world has become dehumanised. Man
feels himself to be isolated in the cosmos
. . . No wonder the Western world feels
uneasy, for it does not know . . . what it has
lost through the destruction of its numi-
nosities. Its moral and spiritual tradition
has collapsed and has left a worldwide
disorientation and dissociation. (1977, pp.
254–255)

Arguably our dissociation lies at the root of our current ecological and social crisis: we believe we can consume and pollute as if there were no consequences, not unlike the addict who continues "using" regardless of bodily damage. There is, now, an increasing awareness of the emptiness of consumerism and a sense that we have sold our soul in exchange for economic development. Further, that among the many devastating effects of our current ecological and social crisis are a range of mental health issues such as depression, anxiety, addictions, relationship failures, narcissism, and more, affecting not only adults but children too.

The psychotherapy profession has done a great deal to explore, articulate, and heal human relationships but still fails to acknowledge, or include, the effects of being displaced from land and disconnected from the earth. Sometimes we can only recognise the deep impact this severance from the earth has had on our psyches when looking through the eyes of others who have grown up in an entirely different culture which is still embedded in the land. A view of white people as they arrive in Turtle Island (the land of North America as described by some Native American peoples) is described here by the relatives of author and activist Jeannette Armstrong of the Okanagan tribe:

"My grandmother said (translated from Okanagan), 'The people down there are dangerous, they are all insane.' My father agreed, commenting, 'It's because they are wild and scatter anywhere.'" Armstrong continues: "If I were to interpret/transliterate the Okanagan meaning of my grandmother's words, it might be this: 'The ones below who are not of us [as place], may be a chaotic threat in action; they are all self-absorbed [arguing] inside each of their heads.' My father's words might be something like this: 'Their actions have a source, they have displacement panic, they have been pulled apart from themselves as family [generational sense] and place [as land/us/survival]'" (Armstrong, 1995, pp. 317, 319).

White settlers are a specific group of people; yet perhaps this powerful description applies to a great number of people in modern culture and speaks to the diagnosis of *dissociation and disorientation* offered by Jung. While psychotherapy offers a practice of healing for the dissociation from self and other humans, the practices of ecopsychology seek to repair a lost connection with the rest of nature in the hope of healing the body–mind, retrieving the soul and restoring the earth (Roszak, Kanner, & Gomes, 1995). The point is, we have a *relationship* with the rest of nature. In the words of eco-theologian Thomas Berry, "The universe is a communion of subjects not a collection of objects" (Berry, 2006, p. 149).

ECOPSYCHOLOGY AND CULTURAL NARRATIVES

The root of our dissociation from nature has a long and complex history. In his major work *Civilization and Its Discontents* Freud wrote:

> *The principal task of civilization . . . is to defend us against nature . . . There are the elements which seem to mock at all human control; the earth which quakes and is torn apart and buries all human life and its works; water, which deluges and drowns everything in turmoil . . . With these forces nature rises up against us, majestic, cruel*

*and inexorable; she brings to our mind
once more our weakness and helplessness,
which we thought to escape through the
work of civilization. (1930, pp. 15–16)*

Here Freud describes the position that Western culture has come to occupy; there is a fight *against* nature with the potential for humiliation if the apparent "battle" is felt to be lost. This lies at the heart of our cultural narrative, which some call The Myth of Progress, familiar to those of us with a Western education. Cultural historian Richard Tarnas describes this story as, "[A] long heroic journey from a primitive world of dark ignorance, suffering, and limitation to a brighter modern world of ever-increasing knowledge, freedom and well-being . . . made possible by the sustained development of human reason and . . . the emergence of the modern mind" (Tarnas, 2007, p. 12). In other words, it's all about onwards and upwards.

ANTHROPOCENTRISM

This history has led us to a place where we see ourselves as separate from, and superior to, all other forms of life.

Other writers use terms such as, "The Story of Separation" (Eisenstein, 2018) or that we are suffering from "separation sickness" (Breytenbach, 2012). Nature – both nature out there as well as our own human nature – is seen as wild, brutal, and in need of control. A power hierarchy exists where the other-than-human world is seen as a collection of resources or objects to be used by humans. The oppression of the non-human world is called anthropocentrism, or human supremacy. Deep ecologist John Seed wrote, "Anthropocentrism . . . means human chauvinism. Similar to sexism, but substitute 'human race' for 'man' and 'all other species' for 'woman'" (1988, p. 35). Anthropocentrism is linked with all other forms of oppression, such as racism, sexism, and classism (Seed, ibid.; Prentice, 2003, pp. 35–36). Certain peoples are seen as closer to the earth with a "lower", more animal nature. For some this justifies their domination and abuse; the genocide of Indigenous peoples, the trans-Atlantic slave trade, and the oppression of women are three examples of this. It is this collection of oppressions that enables capitalism to function.

We are now more familiar with the psychological mechanisms that enable human oppressions to become part of our internal world. For example, women often lack self-confidence as a result of internalising the cultural view that women are of less value than men; people of colour may feel inferior to white people as a result of internalising racism. We have yet to understand more clearly how we internalise anthropocentrism: how the wisdom of the body is devalued, how intuition is dismissed as irrational nonsense, how the senses are seen to lead us astray; in total, how the qualities of our embodied, creaturely self are seen as less than the intellectual reasoning mind. I will return to anthropocentrism, and the ways it manifests in therapy practice, in Chapter 5.

THE CLASH OF TWO STORIES

Those of us who have grown up within the Western mindset struggle with two apparently opposing stories embedded within our psyche. On the one hand there is a narrative about achieving mastery and success through domination and control of nature, including our own nature. To a great extent this story is about a work *against* nature. On the other hand, we see the shoots emerging of a new story, which is in fact a long-known ancient story embedded in our bones, about how to work and live *with* nature. The burning question is how we live this ancient story within the context of modern times. To some extent these two stories simply reflect the ways in which we openly embrace life versus being fearful of and defending against it. Inevitably both attitudes are present. For a variety of complex reasons modern culture has come to be in the grip of fearfulness, or defensiveness, manifesting in the building of walls or the amassing of weapons capable of destroying the earth many times over, or the desire to have control over, or colonise "the other".

In his book *Edge of the Sacred* public intellectual David Tacey draws on Jung's thinking to describe three stages of apprehending the world. In stage one, the land is sacred and spirits of the earth are seen as real forces in the world. In stage two, where we are now, these forces are seen as irrational and mere projections of the mind upon inanimate phenomena "usually to be traced back to hysterical ideas or unruly emotions" (Tacey, 2009, p. 26). While much has been achieved with the scientific, analytic mind, Tacey sees stage two thinking as responsible for the ecological crisis and calls for a stage three thinking in which the world is once again sacred. He writes: "Stage two thinking lands us in a spiritual and emotional wasteland, in which reason and science have cleansed the world of all projections, leaving nothing left in the world for us to relate to, or form spiritual bonds with . . . No longer sacred, it becomes real estate or 'natural resource' to be used to satisfy egotistical desires" (ibid., p. 27). As we enter into stage three thinking Tacey suggests we are becoming open again to the transpersonal forces of the earth and world, but we need cosmologies appropriate to modern times.

Several decades ago, eco-theologian Thomas Berry urged our culture to find a new story to live by. He wrote: "It is all a question of story. We are in trouble just now because we do not have a good story. We are in between stories. The old story – the account of how the world came to be and how we fit into it – is no longer functioning properly, and we have not yet learned the New Story" (Berry, 1978, p. 77). Many writers in the field of ecopsychology suggest that if we can "reconnect with nature", or "fall in love with nature again", our destructiveness of the other-than-human world will cease. Others suggest that deep healing of human culture is far more complex. Jungian analyst

Jerome Bernstein writes that Indigenous cultures live in "reciprocity" psyche and that now we are in the grip of "dominion" psyche, similar to Tacey's stage one and two thinking. Bernstein suggests that rather than moving into a new story, or going back to something in the past, we need to bring reciprocity and dominion psyches into relationship in order to evolve beyond modernity (Bernstein, 2005). This is very difficult when the rational, analytic mind devalues stage one thinking, seeing it as irrational, superstitious, or childlike. Attempts to build bridges between these two ways of thinking appear in the writings of, for example, Carl Jung (1977, pp. 261–271), Rupert Sheldrake (1990), and Robin Wall Kimmerer (2013).

Psychotherapy is part of the new story by bringing emotional intelligence into relationship with the rational mind and by helping individuals to work with their own nature. However, there are several ways in which it has also been caught in the old story. It does not yet recognise that we are in relationship with the more-than-human world from the very beginning of our lives and the impact these wider relationships have on child development as well as on human trauma and healing. It also tends to individualise human trauma, often failing to see the connections between mental illness and the culture we all swim in.

THE MANY MANIFESTATIONS OF SEPARATION SICKNESS – AND ITS HEALING

Inevitably there are multiple ways in which the imbalances and dysfunctionality in our culture manifest within the individual. Ecopsychologists have offered many different insights into our collective condition and how this is lived out in individual sicknesses (for summary see e.g., Prentice, 2003, pp. 39–40). For example, one of the stories of how our separation from nature began is described by Paul Shepard in his seminal book *Nature and Madness* (1982). He suggests that the beginnings of agriculture and domestication marked a turning point in human psychological history. As a result of our gradual domination of nature we suffered the loss of a wild tribal childhood and its traditional rites of passage. Consequently Western culture fails to fully mature into adulthood, and we are left "ontogenetically crippled". Over the course of time we have become an adolescent culture, struggling with fantasies of omnipotence, narcissism, ambivalence, and resulting aggression. This is one of many answers to a central question which ecopsychology raises: why are we so destructive towards the ecosystem which supports us?

Other ecopsychologists offer differing insights: Chellis Glendinning believes that Western culture is suffering from "original trauma" caused by the systematic removal of our lives from nature and being removed from the "life force itself" (Glendinning, 1995, p. 37). Her book title, *My Name is Chellis and I'm in Recovery from Western Civilisation* (1994) suggests an Alcoholics Anonymous-style stepping out of denial into recovery from the traumas of technology and other Western addictions. In the same vein, Albert LaChance (1991) wrote a twelve-step manual for recovery from ecological destructiveness. I have likened consumerism to a giant, collective eating problem (Rust, 2005, 2008b) where recovery is not a carbon diet, but rather an awareness of hunger, longings, and how we become satisfied at a deeper level.

When we are educated to think that the earth is there as a collection of resources for our use, it is little wonder that narcissism is on the rise; when entry into adulthood is marked by material acquisitions and career success, and when the future is so radically uncertain, is it surprising that so many young people suffer from mental health problems or turn to crime? When our wild selves are too domesticated, living an indoor life at the screen, we lose a vital source of life and connection leading to loneliness and isolation with a raft of relationship difficulties and an epidemic of addictions. When we live in such a divided, unequal society, and those in power deny that we are on a reckless path towards ecocide, no wonder people feel rootless, untethered, dissociated, displaced, traumatised, no wonder we see a rise in madness in our society.

Recently ecopsychologist Zhiwa Woodbury has suggested that climate change would better be described as "climate trauma" due to receiving more and more alarming news of this apocalyptic crisis unfolding in our world. One of the reasons we are so unable to face this is because of the backlog of undigested intergenerational trauma (Woodbury, 2019). Clearly, so many of us are suffering from overwhelm. When wounds cannot be faced and healed, inevitably people are drawn to whatever ways of coping they can find, such as denial, addiction, distraction, collusion, and hidden despair. The trauma is then passed on through the generations. Conversely, as the many practices of psychological and spiritual healing spread around the world there can be joy and empowerment in taking the stance that the "trauma stops here, with me". Healing ourselves and our ancestral lines opens out into the wish to heal our relationship with the earth and future generations.

By now I hope it is clear to the reader that out of the field of ecopsychology come a diverse range of ecotherapy practices which centre upon deepening our relationship with the other-than-human world; some offer "nature reconnection" while others also pay attention to our cultural conditioning. David Kidner described the "colonization of the psyche" and the need to "resymbolize nature" (Kidner, 2001). Romanyshyn (2011) called for a therapy of culture and Alastair McIntosh described a cultural psychotherapy (2008, pp. 210–244). The Natural Change Project is a unique example of an attempt to enable nature reconnection at an organisational level, paying attention to culture and nature as well as organisational culture (Kerr & Key, 2012b). Many other ecotherapies are for individuals and groups, with the belief that when you heal the individual you heal the culture. Indeed, part of the work of cultural psychotherapy can be seen as the decolonisation of the mind: the healing of many internalised oppressions and seeing how they interrelate. In Chapter 6 I will return to look at the different ways in which ecopsychotherapeutic insights and practice are being offered in the community. With this in mind, I will now outline some key terms and concepts that are helpful to ecopsychotherapy and point to some of the challenges that lie within the field.

THE ECOLOGICAL SELF

A central part of healing our disconnection from the land is re-conceiving how we experience the self. The term "ecological self" was first coined by deep ecologist Arne Naess. He argues that we enrich and deepen our experience of self through our capacity to identify with others – other humans as well as other species. Through this we can feel compassion and empathy for the other and a sense of ecological identity (Naess, 1988). Development of empathy is a crucial part of mental health.

The ecological self is inextricably linked with, and embedded in, the rest of nature, contrary to familiar notions of a skin-encapsulated ego. This can be an experience of self which is ancient or timeless, which

Joanna Macy describes as a sense of "deep time"; she wrote, "To make the transition to a life-sustaining society we must retrieve that ancestral capacity . . . we need to attune to the longer ecological rhythms and nourish a strong, felt connection with past and future generations" (Macy & Young Brown, 1998, p. 136). For some this might be connecting with stone (see Jung quote on page 39-40 in this text) or "thinking like a mountain" (Leopold, 1949, pp. 129–130). Or it might be an experience of expanding outwards, into the land, as Jung described in his autobiography. "At times I feel like I am spread out over the landscape and inside things, and am myself living in every tree, in the splashing of the waves, in the clouds and the animals that come and go, in the procession of the seasons" (1961, p. 225). This offers a profoundly nourishing experience of oneness with life. It might also support a shift from the suffering of the ego to identification with a larger body with a wholly different sense of time, wonder, and meaning.

Jeannette Armstrong described an Indigenous view of self, making clear that we are interconnected and interdependent with the rest of life with no strict dividing line between self and world:

*We survive within our skin inside the rest
of our vast selves . . . Okanagans teach that
our flesh, blood and bones, are Earth-body;
in all cycles in which the earth moves, so
does our body . . . Our word for body literally means "the land-dreaming capacity"
. . . The Okanagan teaches that emotion
or feeling is the capacity whereby community and land intersect in our beings and
become part of us. This bond or link is a
priority for our individual wholeness or
well-being. (1995, pp. 320–321)*

This resonates with a more recent view that our bodies are a combination of human cells together with other microorganisms whom we host. We inhabit a system of nested relationships which are interconnected and interdependent. From this view the self is not a static or clearly defined "thing" but more a process.

If we see our inner worlds as microcosms of the outer world, there are many ways in which our capacity to identify with creatures, plants, stone, or water brings alive differing aspects of the ecological self. Many will be familiar with Western astrology which enables us to see the qualities of others reflected in ourselves – such as, the perseverance of the mountain goat, the stubbornness and strength of the bull, the introversion of the crab in its shell, or the stinging penetration of the scorpion, and so on. This kind of symbolism is evident in the dream life of many people. I will return to this in Chapter 5.

THE ECOLOGICAL UNCONSCIOUS

In his book *The Voice of the Earth* Roszak stresses that the repression of ecological awareness is the root of madness in industrial society. He wrote, "Just as it has been the goal of previous therapies to recover the repressed contents of the unconscious, so the goal of ecopsychology is to awaken the inherent sense of environmental reciprocity that lies within the ecological unconscious" (1992, pp. 320–321).

Some ecotherapy practitioners, myself included, suggest that the ecological unconscious can be explored through spending time immersed in the more-than-human world as well as through the dreamworld (Kerr & Key, 2012a).

There is a link, here, with Searles's idea of phylogenetic regression which he describes in his seminal book *The Non-Human Environment in Normal Development and in Schizophrenia* (1960). He argues that regression does not stop at childhood but continues back through evolution. Here, Searles recognises that all aspects of the earth community are to be found internally, that our inner worlds are a microcosm of the macrocosm. However, the idea that we solely regress into those places could imply that they are somehow "lower" than human intelligence.

BIOPHILIA, BIOPHOBIA, AND AMBIVALENCE

The term "biophilia" was first used by Erich Fromm to describe "the passionate love of life and all that is alive" (Fromm, 1973, p. 365). In 1984 biologist E. O. Wilson introduced and popularised *The Biophilia Hypothesis* (1984). He wrote, "We are human in good part because of the particular way we affiliate with other organisms. They are the matrix in which the human mind originated and is permanently rooted, and they offer the challenge and freedom innately sought" (p. 139). Wilson understands biophilia as biologically rooted, but, as Dodds pointed out: "Wilson's biophilia is something that can be learned, encouraged and developed. It refers not to a fixed instinct but an innate tendency towards a connection with the natural world which can be nurtured or not, especially during the crucial stages of child development which are of such interest to psychoanalysts" (Dodds, 2011, p. 78).

Biophobia is not so widely discussed but is arguably one of the roots of our destructiveness towards the other-than-human world. Our increasing disconnection from the other-than-human world leads to unfamiliarity and the tendency to see nature as "other". This can lead to fear of nature, or certain aspects of nature, and this has become widespread. While some fears are justified, there are many which are projections and born out of our need to control and conquer the "dangerous wild other". This has led to a great deal of suffering, such as the appalling treatment of animals in factory farming as well as medical testing, often based on the erroneous belief that animals do not feel pain – they are merely objects.

Psychologically, we could say that we have not yet come to terms with our ambivalent relationship with the rest of nature. Nature as The Great Mother is both the ever generous and bountiful mother as well as the terrible mother who causes suffering and takes lives. In protecting our experience of the good mother earth we tend to "split" resulting in idealisation and denigration of Nature. Idealisation is apparent in phrases such as "I love nature" while rats, slugs, spiders, and viruses are denigrated and receive many unwarranted projections. Perhaps one of the most difficult aspects for Western culture is to accept that we are totally dependent on the earth for all our needs. Being in touch with how small we are in relation to the great body of the earth exposes our vulnerabilities and the fact that we are not in control. This might arouse a sense of humiliation in some, especially for those who experienced early trauma (for further discussion of ambivalence see Jordan, 2009; Dodds, 2011, ch. 7). I will return to these themes as a part of anthropocentrism and its healing in Chapter 5.

ECOPSYCHOLOGY AND LANGUAGE

Imagine reading about the whale **who** swam up the Thames and on reaching London Bridge **she** greeted the waiting crowds; or conversely, reading about Susan,

which went for a walk and on reaching the beach **it** lay down for a rest. This is just one illustration of how the story of separation is embedded in our mindset and language; in this case, we see how we refer to non-humans as objects by using "it" and "which" whereas humans are seen as subjects. We also talk about "going out into nature" and use phrases such as "humans and nature" – or, worse, "man and nature" – which imply we are apart from nature.

Ecopsychologist Robert Greenway has emphasised the need to ground ecopsychology in a language that challenges dualism; he suggests that a language for recovery would need to include the poetic (Greenway, 2009). We also need a more relational language. Just as the past 100 years of psychotherapy has created ways to describe the multitude of inner world states and interpersonal dynamics, so the diverse range of ecotherapies are starting to create new languages for our relationship with Nature. This is not necessarily straightforward. New terms such as the "other-than-human world" or the "more-than-human world" (Abram, 1997) are helpful but can be cumbersome and might seem rather pretentious to some. Other new words emerging in popular culture include solastalgia, the distress resulting from environmental change (Albrecht, 2007); terrapsychology, encountering and re-engaging with the soul of place, including the city (Chalquist, 2007); flygsham, a Swedish term meaning flight-shame; eco-anxiety, the rise in anxiety due to multiple environmental crises (Buzzell & Edwards, 2009); nature deficit disorder, the wide range of behavioural problems which arise in children who spend less time outdoors (Louv, 2005).

It can be confusing that we have just the one word "nature" which covers so many different meanings. Nature can be used to describe plants, animals, rocks, landscape, and all features of the world that are not created by humans. Nature can also mean our intrinsic human nature or essence. The root of the word nature is the Latin *natus* meaning birth; it is our birthplace as a species as well as the place to which we return at the end of life. No wonder that for some, including Indigenous peoples, Nature is not just a physical body but sacred also, often signified by using a capital "N" meaning the greater whole in which we live, the web of life, the Great Mystery, the force that is responsible for life. Here, too, I am fumbling for words to describe the ineffable, the divine, none of them quite fitting. We need more nuanced words to match our experience and imaginations.

Ironically, many older words, which emerge from centuries of observation and living with trees, ice, mountains, and the land, are leaving our dictionaries. "Ammil", a Devon term for the thin film of ice that lacquers all leaves, twigs, and grass blades when a freeze follows a partial thaw, and that in sunlight can cause a whole landscape to glitter, is one of countless words which reveal the fine observation by those who are immersed in the daily cycles and transformations of water. This rapid loss of vocabulary has been chronicled by nature writer Robert Macfarlane (2015), who calls for a re-wilding of our language. He also notes the culling of more everyday words from the Oxford Junior dictionary which are no longer felt to be relevant to a modern-day childhood, such as bluebell, acorn, buttercup and dandelion, whereas new additions are terms such as blog, broadband, celebrity and voicemail (Macfarlane, 2015, pp. 3–4). This is yet another illustration of how language mirrors the changes in our lives. Ralph Waldo Emerson described language as "fossil poetry", containing within it the layers of human relational history (Waldo Emerson, 1844, p. 13).

ECOPSYCHOLOGY AS A WHITE, MIDDLE-CLASS COMMUNITY

Ecopsychology has long been criticised for being a predominantly white, privileged community. Architect Carl Anthony is an African American who offers some helpful critiques of ecopsychology and the environmental movement as a whole. He wrote:

> *I think of my next-door neighbor, a woman of seventy years old: her parents were sharecroppers who were driven off the soil in the South by . . . mechanization and the boll weevil . . . [as well as] the Ku Klux Klan and the inability to go to the polls and vote. If you search the pages of ecological literature, you don't find anything about that kind of pain. People in that situation are generally not the people being reached by the Deep Ecologists. Deep Ecology is in touch with something, but the desire of a tiny fraction of middle- and upper-middle-class Europeans to hear the voice of the Earth could be, in part, a*

*strategy by people in these social classes
to amplify their* own *inner voice at a time
when they feel threatened, not only by the
destruction of the planet, but also by the
legitimate claims of multicultural communities clamoring to be heard . . . Why is it
so easy for these people to think like mountains and not be able to think like people of
color? (1995, pp. 264–265, 273)*

Anthony suggested that, "We have to find a way
to build a multicultural self that is in harmony with an
ecological self. We need to embrace human diversity
in the way we deal with each other – as opposed to
the notion that white people are the mainstream and
everyone else is 'other.' An ecopsychology that has
no place for people of color, that doesn't deliberately
set out to correct the distortions of racism, is an oxy-
moron" (ibid., p. 277). (See Prentice, 2001 for a fuller
discussion of these issues.)

4

Psychological responses to ecological crisis

In the following two chapters I will return to the traditional setting of the therapy room to show the many and varied ways in which our relationship with the other-than-human world enters into therapy sessions. In this chapter I will focus on ecological crisis: how clients speak (or don't speak) about their grief and fears and how we respond as therapists. I will show how the unpacking of "eco-anxiety" can go in many different directions, such as the parallel process of grief for human and non-human, our relationship with the land, and the tricky question of where to find hope in this most challenging time.

My client, Amber, arrived glowing from the recent long spell of hot weather but started the session with some concern about the unusually high temperatures for spring. She paused for a few seconds and looked at me, as if to gauge my response. When I reflected back, "You're concerned about the weather?" she nodded and continued to talk at length about how grim the future looks: the world seems so unstable at the moment and the shift to the right in many countries is very worrying. "Then there is Trump", she concluded, "with his denial of climate change I just think we're completely fucked." I discovered that Amber had been harbouring these thoughts about the future for a while, yet this was the first time she had admitted this to anyone, even to herself.

Amber had come to therapy for help with her eating problem and had spent the first two years focusing mostly on inner world issues and her relationship patterns. When I asked her how she felt about climate change she could identify a range of emotions: fear, grief, anger, overwhelm, and powerlessness. She felt guilty living her privileged life when others are so clearly suffering; what could she *do*? When she changed the subject to work difficulties, I acknowledged how overwhelming her feelings about the world might be and perhaps it was particularly hard to stay with feelings of guilt. I then asked her whether these feelings surface at particular times.

She told me the evenings are difficult, after work. The previous night a special item on climate change and migration had triggered an episode of binge eating; watching so many people being torn from their lands reminded her of when she was eleven years old and her family relocated from a place of wide open deserts and lush oases to damp, grey London suburbs: a sharp contrast. No one spoke about this devastating loss the whole family had suffered.

Amber had told me her story when she first arrived in therapy, but now she was ready to feel her grief for the land and community she had lost. She described the desert as an awe-inspiring place in which she felt expanded and that "the space out there had helped to find a peaceful space inside". Looking back, she felt that this had given her a sense of reverence for the earth.

She realised that no one in her family had helped her to digest her grief in this new and very unfamiliar place of London. Her solution at the time was to numb herself through comfort eating, displacing her distress into her relationship to her body. As she grieved for the lost land of her childhood Amber slowly began to feel more present inside her body. By chance she was given a share of a local allotment where growing her own food became a source of great inner nourishment. She discovered that tuning in to her body helped her to tune in to the plants and the land; for example, when she closed her eyes and held seeds in her hand they would show her where, and at what depth, they needed to be planted. Her body was becoming an ally rather than an enemy. Developing her intuitive sense supported the inner work of therapy, as she gradually let go of her addiction to food in favour of *relationships* with human and non-human. Recently she became a volunteer for a local urban farm project. Amber identifies as mixed race and here she has found a multicultural community of people sharing their feelings about global crisis, which has eased her feelings of isolation.

Over the course of time we have returned to her conclusion that "we're completely fucked". How does she imagine the future? The most troubling thing for her is The Great Uncertainty: we can be certain we are facing very troubled times ahead, but when, how, where? Will we survive as a species? She concludes there is no safe place. The questions, "What sustains her through Radical Uncertainty?", "Where does she find her faith?" are ongoing explorations. Her stand-up comedy classes have helped her to find her inner fool, what it means to step off the cliff and surrender to the unexpected in the present moment.

REFLECTIONS ON THIS PROCESS

It is striking how a brief comment about the weather, so easily passed by, can reveal existential fears about the future. Jungian analyst Thomas Singer wrote: "Extinction anxiety is flooding the planet, although it frequently expresses itself in a displaced form of group or cultural anxiety rather than in the direct experience of the fear of extinction" (2018, p. 205). He suggests this is different from annihilation anxiety, a deep fear of threats to one's individual survival. Extinction anxiety may contribute to addictions, anxieties, and other mental health problems. I have written elsewhere about a client who was using drugs and alcohol to numb her previously unexpressed anxiety about the state of the planet (Rust, 2008a). Psychotherapist Susan Bodnar wrote, "Carefully considering clinical material of some young adults suggests that aspects of obliterative drinking and dissociative materialism may be enactments of a changing relationship between people and their ecosystems" (2008, p. 484).

ECO-ANXIETY, DENIAL, AND DISAVOWAL

The more general term "eco-anxiety" has been in use for over a decade. Buzzell and Edwards described a range of feelings when someone wakes up to the ecological crisis, such as shock, overwhelm, despair, and the temptation to retreat into a state of denial (2009, pp. 123–130). As this example with Amber shows, a range of feelings lie beneath eco-anxiety. Deep ecologist Joanna Macy was one of the first to suggest that we need to "honour our pain for the world", naming and exploring the feelings that surface and – very importantly – that need to be shared as a community. She emphasises that our emotional responses are part of a healthy response-ability to a catastrophic eco-crisis; allowing the feelings to flow means that we can move from a state of numbness and apathy to feeling empowered into action, in her words "from despair to empowerment". She has developed a set of practices known as "The Work that Reconnects" (Macy & Young Brown, 1998).

Apathy is often used to account for the state of paralysis that we are gripped by, unable to take action in the face of such an urgent crisis; this has been misinterpreted as lack of care. In fact, the great majority of people do care very much about the earth and our futures but they may be paralysed by intense feelings that they are unable to process (Lertzman, 2015). Equally they may feel overwhelmed by the scale of the problems we face, so it is not always obvious what action to take; this situation has further been confused by misinformation spread by those invested in fossil fuels (Hamilton, 2010).

Disavowal is a helpful term to describe how many people know the alarming facts of climate change but turn a blind eye in order to continue with everyday life; the anxiety-provoking reality is split off from consciousness, preventing us from making a response to emergency. This is to be distinguished from a state of denial which is refuting the facts of climate change (Weintrobe, 2012, pp. 33–46). Naming these different states helps both therapist and client, acknowledging the difficulty we all have in facing climate change.

"MY CLIENTS DON'T TALK ABOUT CLIMATE CHANGE"

Many psychotherapists say their clients do not mention climate change. There will, of course, always be people who do not wish to bring world events into their therapy sessions. But there may also be reasons why clients do wish to voice their fears. For some, climate change is frightening, even traumatic. Trauma is often split off from consciousness and buried; it may reappear in dreams or in offhand remarks, as the client both does and does not want to speak about it. If a therapist has explored their own process in relation to the earth and eco-crisis, it becomes easier to pick up the clues, such as offhand comments about unusual weather, remarks about other political disturbances which may lead to fears of climate change, or references to love for the land and other-than-human world which may then give rise to anxiety and/or grief. Sometimes eco-anxiety is buried beneath other psychological disturbances such as addictions. Since there has been virtually no inclusion of our relationship with the earth in psychotherapy trainings, many therapists may well not pick up these clues and feel ill-equipped to know how to respond.

The client may fear that their anxieties will be interpreted as really about some other personal matter (displacement anxiety). The psychotherapy profession has a long history of looking for the personal behind all political material brought to the session, although there will, of course, be times when this is true (Samuels, 1993, p. 116; Totton, 2016, p. 15). Some therapists may also believe that the climate crisis has been exaggerated and this may be picked up by the client who then fears to speak out. Taking action is frequently suggested as a helpful response to eco-anxiety, yet it may take time for the emotional responses to be unpacked and digested. If action comes too soon, from a place of "should" rather than from the heart, this can be a recipe for burnout.

There is no prescription for dealing with eco-anxiety in therapy. Every client is different and, as I have shown here, once the emotional responses have been unpacked, and the anxiety respected in its own right, the process may flow in many different directions, sometimes triggering issues from the past.

RELATIONSHIP WITH LAND AND PLACE

David Tacey grew up in Alice Springs, amongst Aboriginal peoples. He has described how, in their cosmology, "Landscape is a mythopoetic field . . . at the centre of everything: at once the source of life, the origin of the tribe, the metamorphosed body of blood-line ancestors and the intelligent force which drives the individual and creates society . . . In the western frame . . . if landscape is felt to possess a certain character or mood, this is said to be created by the perceiving subject and projected upon the land" (Tacey, 2009, pp. 145–146).

The prevailing attitude in our culture sees nature as having no soul, a backdrop to human affairs. Yet despite this, many people have deep experiences in relation to the land. Amber's love for, and attachment to, place is not unusual: many people describe falling in love with a particular place and the importance of home – whether it is in forests or mountains or by the sea (Rust, 2014). Others describe different qualities or atmospheres of place, including vestiges of ancestral trauma being held in the land. Many peoples are driven mad when they are torn from or forced out of their homelands. Many never find their place of "home".

Our relationship to place and the land, both rural and urban, is vital to our psyche, yet this often goes unmentioned in the course of therapy. Depth psychologist Craig Chalquist describes a range of ways in which our relationship with the land, which he calls "terrapsychology", emerges through dreams, myths, and stories (Chalquist, 2007), well known to Indigenous peoples and their cosmologies.

I have focused, here, on the earth-related aspects of Amber's therapy yet this was very much interwoven with her ongoing intrapsychic work. This illustrates that ecopsychotherapy is not just the work of responding to eco-anxiety, or moments of love for the land. Our relationships with the more-than-human world are woven into, and inseparable from, relationships with self, family, culture, and the earth.

GRIEF FOR THE EARTH AND PARALLEL PROCESS

For some people a deep relationship with the more-than-human world can be life-saving when their family life is dysfunctional. My client John spent much of his time outdoors in his early years, escaping from rows between his parents which frequently led to his father being violent towards his mother. As an adult John became an environmentalist; eventually he sought therapy when he became depressed and burnt out. He began by telling me about his concerns for the earth. As the grief came pouring out, he realised how angry he was with humans, saying, "The earth would be better off without us". As he explored this further he could see that his rage wasn't helping his campaign work. It was only after he had spent time exploring his passionate feelings about our human abuse of the earth that he was then able to vent his anger towards his father for his abuse of his mother, and the guilt he felt for being unable to protect her.

At this point John told me that his previous therapist had made an interpretation that his need to protect the earth was really about his wish to repair his failed attempts as a child to protect his mother from his father's violence. He could now see that there might be some truth in this, but at the time it felt as though his grief for the earth wasn't being respected in its own right. Once these different layers of feelings had become disentangled he was able to feel some compassion towards his father for the trauma he'd experienced in World War II and his violent behaviour which followed.

Returning to the present-day situation, John began to understand why so many people couldn't hear the emergency of the earth: there was too much undigested trauma, creating a collective numbness and apathy. This insight, gained during a long period of time in therapy, helped his work as an activist. John's story shows the importance of following the client in their grief: he needed to start with his grief for the earth, and his rage towards humans, before he could face his troubled relationships with his family. This parallel process between family and earth relationships gave him insights into each realm. In the next example the client follows a different parallel process with her grief.

GRIEF FOR THE EARTH: ANIMAL HELPERS

Carol complained of feeling rather bored with therapy; several times she wondered whether she was ready to end. I wasn't sure; but since she had been seeing me for some time, and had already been in long-term therapy previously, I began to wonder whether she was right. When I voiced this, quick as a flash she experienced my remark as cruel, a repeat of her cruel mother in childhood. However, this exchange went underground as various dramas in Carol's family took over. A few sessions later, I noticed a queen hornet crawling across the chair. This large, yellow and black queen became a potent symbol for Carol's stinging mother and helped us to return to what had happened between us. The queen's appearance sparked Carol's anger with me about my remark, the first time she had found her power in her anger towards me. What had been hiding behind her boredom with therapy now became clearer: she was reluctant to tackle her feelings about her cruel mother – and, it seems, so was I! But Carol's anger with me helped to release her poisonous rage with her mother. Eventually, to her amazement, she discovered some forgiveness of this woman who was now quite old and dementing. She was then able to start grieving for the mother whom she never had.

Two months later Carol arrived in floods of tears. After our last session she had arrived home to find the shocking sight of a dead duck who had flown into the window of their house and tragically broken her neck. Carol was utterly distraught and sobbed in a way she hadn't done for years. She had been aware of the ecological crisis for a long time, but only now was she able to feel the depths of her pain about the multiple losses to the web of life, the fears for her children's future, the needless plastic everywhere, and so much more. She gathered up the still-warm duck and held her close, honouring her life and offering profound gratitude for the entry into deep grief that this creature had offered through her death.

Carol then entered a long depression – an unfamiliar state for her as a "doing" person. During this time, she was able to explore the depths of her despair about her relationship with the earth and the parallels with her relationship with her mother.

Unlike John, Carol needed to start with her rage and grief towards her mother, before she could feel the depths of her despair about the earth. In both cases, the parallel processes were helpful.

Summarising people's stories in this way can give a rather unrealistic view of such journeys into the underworld of despair, rage, and grief which are inevitably very long and painful and, like the weather, never follow a linear path. In a culture which is so obsessed with the heroic "onwards and upwards" motto of progress, we resist the downwards and backwards part of the journey. Yet it is only when we join "on-wards and upwards" together with "backwards and downwards" that we can make the circular journey that nature teaches.

Amber, John, and Carol were able to re-emerge again bearing gifts from the night, which gave them renewed capacity to enter the next stage of their lives. However, many people may get stuck in grief along the way, becoming bitter, angry, and chronically depressed, turning away from life and unable to love. In her paper "Loss and Climate Change" psychotherapist Rosemary Randall reviewed a number of theories about loss, suggesting that "The work of grief is a series of tasks that can be embraced, refused, tackled or abandoned . . . always in progress, never complete . . . The work may falter or stall, the bereaved person may abandon their attempt at recovery, take heart again, move forward and so on" (2009, p. 121). Randall offers an adapted version of Worden's "tasks of grief": accepting the reality of the loss (or going into denial); working through the painful emotions of grief (or shutting off emotionally); adjusting to the new environment/developing a new sense of self (or not adapting, becoming helpless, bitter, angry, withdrawing); reinvesting emotional energy (or refusing to love, turning away from life). She then suggests this way of naming our grieving process may be helpful in understanding our many and varied responses to climate change.

5

Exploring anthropocentrism

In this chapter I will look at some of the ways in which anthropocentrism – the view that humans are superior to the rest of nature and the oppression that results from this – comes into the work of psychotherapy. This might include the taking back of unwanted parts of the self which are cast onto the other-than-human world, and the painful process of reintegration; exploring the ways in which we are in conflict with our own "creatureliness" – how capacities such as intuition, emotional intelligence, our capacity to be grounded and live in the world of the senses – may be diminished in the face of the domination of the analytic mind. Bringing these different and often conflicting parts of the self into relationship gives us the chance to become fully human again and challenges our very identity as human beings.

RELATIONSHIPS WITH ANIMAL COMPANIONS

My client, Jenny, arrived for her second session and immediately started to sob uncontrollably. She told me that her beloved dog Gem was dying. "But", she added cautiously, "you must think I'm very silly to be so upset about a dog; after all, *she's only an animal.*" I asked Jenny to tell me more about Gem. They had known each other for fourteen years, walked together most days, and lived through so many ups and downs. Gem had been such a loyal and loving companion, the thought of losing her was unbearable. Yet her fear that I would judge her grief as an overreaction is part of a cultural attitude where animal companions are seen as "less important" than humans. Far from being "less important", relationships between animals and humans are frequently experienced as deep connections, offering many different qualities, regardless of their being two different species. Jenny described how her relationship with Gem was the first time she had received unconditional love; this was therefore a very profound relationship. It is not unusual for humans to experience such a deep love in their relationships with animal companions.

RELATIONSHIPS WITH THE ANIMAL SELF

My client, Gloria, whom I had been seeing for a long time, arrived very distressed; on her way to therapy some white youths had leaned out of a car and shouted "Monkey, monkey" at her, making some insulting gestures. Naturally she was profoundly shocked – and so was I. It was some years since she had been on the receiving end of such blatant racism although as a black woman she was used to frequent and demeaning micro-incidents of racism, which can easily go unnoticed by white people. After she talked about her experiences of racism at length, and the session was nearing an end, she smiled as she reflected further on this incident. "You know what," she said, "the funny thing is that I love monkeys and the great apes. They're often seen as stupid animals – but actually, they're intelligent and quite beautiful. They are definitely *not* subhuman! I guess those young, working-class, white guys are often seen as stupid in our society, and maybe they were using me, as a black woman, to get rid of their feelings of shame – shame of feeling less than others, or even of feeling less than human." By making this move she stepped out of identifying with the racist and anthropocentric (and possibly sexist!) projection cast onto her.

There are many ways in which humans cast their unwanted feelings onto "the other"; men onto women, black onto white, middle-class onto working class, and humans onto animals. Part of cultural healing is the inner work of dealing with projections: the oppressor must re-own what she or he has cast out and the oppressed must somehow remove what they have internalised. But this is not a straightforward process. For example, acknowledging my own white racism is not easy: there is deep shame in uncovering the ways in which my white privilege operates. It can be equally difficult to unravel the many ways in which we repeatedly use and abuse the rest of nature. Many of our projections are embedded in our language, phrases such as "stupid cow", "greedy pig", or "they were drunk, out of control, behaving like animals" are in everyday use. All of these are human judgements according to *our* value system. Gradually, with the help of science and the art of noticing, we are seeing more clearly the unique and diverse intelligences of the more-than-human world; animals are far from stupid. We are also learning that wild has its own order; experiments in "re-wilding" are showing that when nature is left to its own devices, without human interference, regeneration can happen very rapidly (Tree, 2018). Totton suggests that "wild therapy" is a corresponding form of re-wilding humans and human culture (Totton, 2011).

CONFLICTS BETWEEN THE ANALYTIC MIND AND THE BODY–SOUL

My client, Emma, who was struggling with an eating problem, was intent on trying to control her appetite with her rational mind. She hated her body and repeatedly tried to erase her hunger, both physical and emotional. She could manage to get through the day by eating very little but during the evenings, alone at home, she would find herself faced with a range of uncomfortable feelings which she found unbearable. She found her needs repulsive and she coped by bingeing on food. In her dreams a terrifying alien creature appeared, with rows of teeth, bursting out of her stomach, reminiscent of "The Alien" in the sci-fi horror films. This image seemed to personify her regular binge eating. She was so alienated from her needs they now appeared in monstrous form, as if separate from her, having been feared and pushed away for so long.

Part of the therapeutic work was to help Emma re-inhabit her body, to reincarnate, so that she could begin to listen to what her stomach wanted, to *feel*, to distinguish between physical and emotional hunger. As she slowly began to listen to, trust, and then follow her body, rather than to try to control and dominate it, the body was no longer a split-off monstrous creature but an ally in recovery. However, this was a very difficult and arduous process for her. She was frequently in the grip of a very severe analytic, rational part of the self who had no time for feelings or vulnerability, who viewed intuition with deep suspicion, the world of the senses and feelings as time-wasting, and the body as merely a vehicle to carry around her very important mind. In fact, this part of herself was against the whole project of psychotherapy so it was astounding that she managed to come to therapy each week. This attitude had been internalised from both parents. The other part of her – whom she called her "body–soul" – was drawn to paint and to spend time walking by her local river often accompanied by her friend's dog. Her body-soul found the work of therapy invaluable yet was frequently silenced in the face of the rational self and this would take her to a very empty and depressed place inbetween sessions.

Gradually she began to see that, in fact, the rational self was afraid of the body-soul with its apparent messiness, unpredictable feelings, its fluid way of being in the world, with no facts or measurements for reference. It was painstaking work to gradually facilitate a conversation between these two parts of the self. At one stage Emma had a very vivid dream: she was practising some kind of herbalism, a long time ago, when she was caught and sentenced for witchcraft. She awoke at the point of being burnt at the stake, terrified. She realised that her own deep fear of connecting with her intuition came not only from her parents but from many hundreds of years of the persecution of witches; the terror of speaking from our intuitive selves, especially for women, still lives on today in the collective unconscious. It was clear that Emma's inner world was shaped by parental influences, but also by cultural forces. One of the many things that supported her to reconnect with her intuition, her sensual world, and her feelings was her relationship with her animal companion, her local river, and particular trees.

TRANSRATIONAL EXPERIENCES

Jungian analyst Jerome Bernstein uses the term "borderland personalities" to describe those who perceive and receive communications between themselves and plants, animals, rocks, the earth, and the ancestors. A client told Bernstein, "My sensitivities to all things animate and inanimate were with me from my earliest memories. I would touch my bedroom door and it would 'tell' me about the forest it came from" (Bernstein, 2005, p. 85). Another woman described being traumatised by the "sleeping jar" at school. The teacher encouraged pupils to bring in live "specimens" which were put in the jar with an ether-soaked rag at the bottom. They were then pinned on a cork board for viewing. She described how she could hear the bugs dying, "Most made gasping and moaning sounds as the air in the jar was replaced by unbreathable fumes. The butterflies screamed. It was a high-pitched staccato sound" (ibid., p. 92). It was obvious to her that no one else could hear the sounds, but it so traumatised her that she ran to the toilets and put the taps full on to drown out the noises. She was told by her parents to "get over it" and soon afterwards she began developing respiratory problems and eventually pneumonia, during which time she had a powerful out-of-body experience of a deeply spiritual nature. She survived to tell the tale, but after this traumatic event she lost her sensitivities to the non-human world. It was only later in life that her deep connection with the non-human world returned. Her trauma was twofold: first of all, witnessing the distress of the insects, and second, her gift of connection was not believed (ibid.).

Bernstein realised that many clients might not tell their therapist such stories for fear of not being believed or being pathologised. He stresses that their experiences are neither delusional, dissociative, nor hallucinatory. Rather, they are *transrational* experiences. Borderlanders experience more of a oneness with the natural world, rather than a separateness and this is their psychic reality all of the time. In this sense their psychic experience resembles the Indigenous psyche which has never experienced a separation from Nature. This state of consciousness has been described in many ways such as Levi-Bruhl's "participation mystique" (ibid., p. 9) and Owen Barfield's "original participation" (Baring & Cashford, 1991, pp. 435–437).

DREAMS AND ARCHETYPAL POLARITIES

In his paper, "The Eagle and the Serpent: the Minding of Matter" Jungian analyst Roderick Peters described a number of patients' dreams with similar themes in which the same threesome appears: an eagle, a snake, and the dreamer. For example, "A man in his mid-thirties . . . felt a jarring disharmony between his serenely cool, philosophical states of mind and [his] descents into hot-blooded sexuality. [In his dreams] usually he was on a raft, trying to get across a river or lake . . . As he tried to get [the woven raft] over the water, snakes . . . wriggled up through the woven reeds and he felt mortally afraid of them . . . All the time he was aware of the presence of an eagle perched on the top of the mast, which seemed unconcerned with the goings-on below . . . A woman who had no confidence at all in her intellect dreamed of an eagle whose feet were stuck to rock so that it could not fly. Talking about the dream, she said . . . that the rock needed the eagle to be able to fly because otherwise the rock's dreams were earthbound" (Peters, 1987, pp. 359–360).

Peters told how the eagle and serpent stand for archetypal polarities, and that they have always been engaged in an age-old struggle, appearing in stories through the ages as well as in our dreams. "Eagle mind" he described as an experience of flying above things, getting an objective overview, with piercing, focused vision, a place of transcendence, more separate from the earth, associated with the elements of fire, air, and spirit. "Serpent mind" is an experience of being very close to, or inside, the dark earth, a power of a deep and inward kind, piercing and paralysing, a subjective participatory experience associated with water and earth. "Serpent mind [is] of the realm of blood and viscera. This mind is lodged deep in collectivities . . . if I see someone gashed and bleeding, my blood-mind is affected almost as if it were 'my' blood. It is as if there were no boundary between me and that wounded person . . . it is an activity of the ancient mind" (ibid., p. 373). He continued:

> *The experiences of one's bodily self which come when 'I' consciousness allows itself to descend into a participating awareness . . . are our real connection to the past; we can go down and down through the unending evolutionary layers within our bodily nature, and feel a sense of linking up with the dimmest and deepest roots of life. Through it we can know renewal, as if we have touched vitality itself. The descent feels full of dangers because we know we have gone into the power of the old serpent . . . The 'I' [of our conscious experience] . . . is all but submerged in feelings of oneness, oceanic feelings, feelings of isolation, abandonment, eternity, infinity, fear, love, hatred, rage; all the passions in fact. (ibid.)*

This is a fine description of how conflicted we are in relation to Nature. The "I" is terrified of losing itself into the boundlessness of the Great Mystery, becoming one with Nature; yet, as Indigenous peoples have known for thousands of years, when we are able to surrender to this experience of oneness a deep healing can arise.

Peters describes how the relationship between eagle and serpent appears in early stories from around the world. In Norse mythology the eagle and the serpent are to be found *in relationship* in the world tree, the eagle perched on the branches and the snake curled at the roots. As time went on, the eagle gradually became the victor while the snake carried our shadow projections, paralleling the move towards a transcendent spirituality and a rising fear of earth, embodiment, and darkness. For example, in many Christian churches today the eagle is on the lectern carrying the Bible, and the snake is held firmly by its claws, or absent altogether (ibid., pp. 361–364).

There is a fear of regressing down the evolutionary scale into something "primitive" and losing what we believe to be our special human qualities; a fear of being swallowed by something so much larger and more powerful than ourselves, a fear of experiences we cannot explain with the rational mind; a fear of being taken over by the senses, "led up the garden path" unable to think. These are just a few of the many ways in which our fears of the earth and our own earthliness might propel us to transcend into the sky.

The story of the eagle and the serpent mirrors the way in which our dominant culture has been unable to hold the tension between body and mind, earth and sky, ancient and modern, emotion and thought, *eros* and *logos*, matter and spirit polarities that have moved from an equal tension to the domination of one capacity, or quality, over another. This is reflected in our relationships with the more-than-human world, how we relate to our own body and our embodied ways of perceiving the world, such as intuition, instinct, emotion, and our sensual natures.

SUMMARY

Anthropocentrism is the way in which humans denigrate and oppress the other-than-human world. The examples I have described in this chapter show how we are affected by that oppression as individuals. Just as men need to attend to their own internalised sexism, and white people need to attend to their internalised racism, so those of us in industrial growth culture need to attend to the ways in which we internalise anthropocentrism. Healing anthropocentrism is therefore about retrieving our shadow projections from aspects of nature as well as recovering our respect for ourselves as animals. Furthermore, all these oppressions intersect with one another and this is known as intersectionalism.

Ecopsychotherapy: weaving the threads

In this chapter I want to pull together some threads which run throughout this book, reflecting on some of the core principles or qualities within ecopsychotherapy. Other writers have described a set of principles or qualities in related fields, for example: "the eight principles of ecopsychology" (Roszak, 1992, pp. 320–321) and "the qualities of wild therapy" (Totton, 2011, pp. 184–203).

EVERYTHING/EVERYONE IS ALWAYS IN RELATIONSHIP

Ecopsychotherapy recognises that we are part of a larger whole, a living and aware web of life, an animate earth. All beings are interconnected and interdependent and live within reciprocal relationships. We are part of a system of nested relationships. From the start of life, we form relationships with, and attachments to, the other-than human world – land, creatures, plants, elements, place, and more. This is not just an ecological fact but *a psychological experience*. All these relationships – human and non-human – make us who we are as human *beings*. Human healing is inseparable from restoring the earth.

THE ECOLOGICAL SELF AND ECOLOGICAL UNCONSCIOUS

Arising from this ecological reality is a sense of self that is embedded in the land and interwoven with the web of life. Ecopsychotherapy recognises the ecological self and ecological unconscious and is developing a language to describe their relationship to other parts of the self.

EMBODIMENT

Ecopsychotherapy recognises that we are embodied creatures, human animals. Our embodied self is not only our experience through our sensory worlds but through feeling and intuition also. Ecopsychotherapy recognises that all these creaturely aspects of being human need fostering alongside, and in relation to, the intellectual life of the human mind.

HUMAN STORY AND EARTH STORY

Ecopsychotherapy recognises that our human story is always in relation with our earth story. There are many different ways in which our relationship with earth might emerge in the course of therapy: a lifetime of relationships with animals, plants, elements, place; peak experiences in the outdoors; the place that is thought of as "home"; fears of, or trauma relating to, the other-than-human world (experiences of earthquakes, phobias, death of much loved companions, being forced to leave one's homeland due to war or natural disaster); mothers'/fathers' relationships with the other-than-human world; ancestral relationships with land: fears and loves which might run through the generations; relationship with animal self: intuition/feeling; how these relationships emerge in dreams.

THE TRAUMA OF INDUSTRIAL GROWTH CULTURE

Ecopsychotherapy recognises that the dominant culture we inhabit is destroying the web of life. This impacts on our health – including our mental health. A hierarchy has been created, putting white, Western, male, middle-class values at the top. This worldview impacts on, and shapes, our psychological experience creating a culture of humans who see themselves as separate from, and superior to, the rest of life. This hierarchy of values has become internalised and we find ourselves in conflict with ourselves as human animals.

Our experience of being separate from the rest of nature, as well as from our own creatureliness, disconnects us from the source of life, a vital experience of nourishment and oneness. This has created generations of loneliness and isolation into which the great hunger of consumer culture has been born. This is breeding a raft of psychological disturbances which need to be seen in relation to culture rather than individualised and privatised.

TRAUMA AND HEALING IN RELATION TO THE GREATER WHOLE

Ecopsychotherapy recognises that human trauma arises not only from human relationships but from the complex relationships and layers of ecological and intergenerational trauma that surround us. Healing the individual is not just in relation to the human family but in relation to the wider social and ecological family. The ecological self therefore exists in relation to the multicultural self.

ECOPSYCHOTHERAPY IS A HOLISTIC AND DIVERSE PRACTICE

Ecopsychotherapy recognises diversity as an essential part of life. It may be practised in many diverse ways and may draw on a diversity of conceptual frames. Very often it is practised outdoors, bringing our relationship with the other-than-human world into the session; this counters our very indoor-focused lifestyles. However, ecopsychotherapy can also be practised indoors. This combines an awareness of several layers: our relationships with the wider environment, beyond our human family, from our earliest experience; our ancestral relationships with the land; our relationship with our embodied self: intuition, feeling, and the world of the senses and the ways in which this has been culturally denigrated.

THE SHADOW OF ECOPSYCHOTHERAPY

Ecopsychotherapy is a white, middle-class movement which has emerged from the brokenness of white culture. In seeking an earth-related healing practice many ecotherapists draw on the cosmologies and practices of earth-based cultures. We must be aware of, and guard against, cultural appropriation in our ways of thinking and the practices we offer. We must also attend to the inner work of how white privilege operates in our relationships. Otherwise ecopsychology risks being another privilege-dominated movement which overlooks the importance of diversity within its own community and the increased vulnerability to environmental challenges faced by those with less.

ECOPSYCHOTHERAPY TRAINING

In order for the ecopsychotherapeutic process to be unpacked and explored in therapy, the therapist needs to be familiar with their own process in relation to the earth. This includes: knowing your own earth story; spending regular time outdoors in a relational way; knowing what is happening to the earth and enquiring into your own responses; being familiar with your cultural attitudes towards the earth community. Ideally ecopsychotherapy should be a fully integrated part of any training. While that is not the case there are post-qualification trainings available (see www.ecopsychology.org.uk/training for more information).

Ecopsychotherapy in the community

So far, this book has focused on how our relationship with the earth and the more-than-human world needs to become an integral part of psychotherapy. In this chapter I will explore how the insights and practices of psychotherapy might be of help to the collective as we stumble towards creating an ecological civilisation. This is an extremely challenging time when our life-styles and all our decision-making processes, both at home and at work, need to be revisioned. In every area we must prioritise the needs of the web of life rather than allowing human needs to take precedence over the needs of everyone with whom we share our home. There are forces of resistance on this path at every turn. As therapists we know how great the resistance to change can be – we are alert to it every day.

A key question is how people are inspired to act. Is it by presenting yet more alarming facts about the human destruction of the earth or by offering a positive vision of the future if we take xyz action? On the other hand, how might we communicate with those who deny the reality of climate change? Active listening to those seen to occupy "the other side" is a vital skill. There is also a pressing need to take account of emotional process in the actions we take as well as to attend to our deeper relationship with the other-than-human world; if we don't we are likely to reproduce the same psychological dynamics that brought us to this point in the first place. To quote a much-used saying, "We must be the change we want to see". As others have suggested, we need a cultural psychotherapy (McIntosh, 2008, pp. 210–244; Robertson, 2016).

Here are some reflections on some of the questions and dilemmas posed for all of us amidst our unfolding earth crisis, together with some community-based responses.

PSYCHOLOGICAL RESPONSES TO ECOLOGICAL CRISIS

Eco-anxiety is clearly on the rise as alarming news reports echo the scientific research and predictions about our worsening climate chaos. People around the globe are struggling with their emotional responses as floods, fires, and droughts worsen and become more unpredictable. Those on the front line of climate change activism and research need to be alert to the emotional toll of this work and how it might affect or infect the dynamics of working groups. Scientists, for example, have shared just how painful and frightening it is to be aware of what is unfolding. As I have already written in Chapter 4, eco-anxiety is not a pathology, but rather a natural response to an extremely worrying situation. Therefore, unless the anxiety is crippling, it is not a reason to seek therapy. Rather, we need spaces in the community where people can gather to express and process their feelings, with encouragement to take action. The Work That Reconnects (see page 84-85 in this text) was developed by Joanna Macy in the 1980s to do just this (Macy & Young Brown, 1998). There is now a network of facilitators in various countries who offer a set of creative practices which enable people to move from despair to empowerment to take action on behalf of a life-sustaining society. In the past few years Macy's work has emerged in Active Hope groups, developed by Chris Johnstone and others (Macy & Johnstone, 2012). The practice of "active hope" offers hope as a process rather than a state, so that hope and despair do not become polarised. More recently Extinction Rebellion, now a growing movement worldwide, has been offering grief-tending and eco-anxiety workshops with similar intentions. If we do not attend to our emotional responses then we are likely to suffer burnout. Self-care must be part of earth care and vice versa.

In his book *The Wild Edge of Sorrow*, Francis Weller (2015) describes how Western patterns of amnesia and anaesthesia affect our capacity to cope with personal and collective loss. He suggests that there has always been the need to share grief communally for we need the compassion of the group and the container of ritual in order to fully digest our grief, rather than hiding it away in shame.

Created in 2002, Altars of Extinction is one of the many art exhibits which speak to eco-grief. Exhibition curator and psychology professor Mary Gomes wrote, "Altars of Extinction is an artistic and ritual memorial that provides opportunities to collectively contemplate and grieve the extinction of plant, animal and fungal species at human hands. As it moves from location to location, the represented species change to include those local to the region" (2009).

A recent piece of action by Melinda Plesman, who lost her home in the fires in New South Wales, Australia in December 2019, clearly moved the hearts of many. She posted a video in which she described her family home and her love of the land, the forest and the birds, where she had brought up her children. Now it was gone. She collected together some of the charred remains and took them to Canberra, laying them out in front of Parliament House. This was a message to Prime Minister Morrison and his government, many of whom deny the reality of climate change. This was a potent way to transform great personal loss into action for the collective (Cole, 2019).

While some might fear the rise in eco-anxiety, we might re-frame this as an outbreak of sanity. The collective is no longer sleepwalking into ecological crisis, unable to feel. Rather, we are increasingly *feeling* the insanity of what is happening in the world and this is a necessary step towards taking action. The definition of mental health needs to include empathy for the other-than-human world.

CLIMATE CHANGE AND CHILDREN

Many people are asking how we talk to children about the unfolding climate crisis. After all, it is their futures that hang in the balance. Climate activist Greta Thunberg has been extremely successful in inspiring a worldwide youth movement engaged in regular climate strikes, demanding more action from adults and empowering many young people to speak out on this subject. She is careful to point out that many other young activists have been speaking out about environmental crisis for years, such as those from Indigenous communities and people of colour, whose lives have already been impacted; yet sadly their voices have not been listened to by those in power.

Psychotherapist Caroline Hickman has been carrying out research to find out how children feel about climate change because the impact on that age group will be considerable, particularly in poorer countries.

Among the children she has interviewed she has found that they are aware of what is happening and do not want the subject to be glossed over with panaceas, such as "Everything will be OK" (Hickman, 2019, p. 42). She, and others, are offering workshops for children and parents to enable them to express their feelings about what is happening, and to talk in more depth.

Many people are making the choice not to have children at this time. Some do not want to contribute to rising population levels or yet more carbon emissions; others do not wish to bring children into a world with such an uncertain and bleak future. Some women have declared they are on "birth strike" until climate change ends. Psychotherapist Emma Palmer explores the many issues involved in making such monumental life decisions in her book *Other Than Mother* (Kamalamani, 2016).

Child development is profoundly affected by the changes in our relationship with the earth. Many readers will have had personal experience of watching this generation have far less access to outdoor time than the last. What about children who grow up without any meaningful relationship with the other-than-human world? When light pollution means we no longer have access to the starry cosmos? Or when technology takes over from trees as the playmate? Or when parks become the boundaries for gang territories and are no longer safe to play in? Richard Louv (2005) calls this "Nature-Deficit Disorder" and we can only guess at how this might affect the next generation.

In Western culture most children experience a profound split between indoors and outdoors at an early age: when a child is sent to school they are taught that "real" work happens in the classroom while "play" is outdoors. "The environment" becomes a distraction to the focused study at a desk. There are many other forms of splitting: childrens' beds are piled high with fluffy animals, childhood stories are full of creatures who talk, pets are part of the family and are known to experience feelings such as pain, joy, and loss, as humans do. Yet later on we are told that this was an illusion; worse, children are taught to not worry about cruelty to the animals we eat or whom we keep in cages to perform medical experiments on. This dissociation is learned at an early age.

I have given just a few of the many examples of the ways in which our culture influences our connection with the earth from the very beginning of our lives.

Forest schools are one of the many growing initiatives to help children have a meaningful relationship with the other-than-human world from an early age (Birkeland & Aasen, 2012).

HEALING THE SPLIT BETWEEN ACTION AND RE-FLECTION

It is no surprise to discover that among the many splits that exist within Western culture the practical is split from the psychological and relational. For example, many green NGOs would view the process of delving into the inner world as a distraction from effective practical action and at worst self-indulgent and manipulative. In Arnstein's *A Ladder of Citizen Participation* (1969) "therapy" is placed on the second to bottom rung of the ladder of citizen participation – only just above "manipulation" at the bottom! This chart is still used in teaching on participation in NGOs today. This split between action and reflection has its roots in the cultural narrative about fighting against nature; in this case it is about fighting our own nature, as if exploring feelings would lead us astray rather than liberating energy for action in the world.

More recently some movements have begun to heal this split by paying attention to psychological process in the work of environmental action. In 2006 the successful Transition movement began in Devon, UK and spread to many parts of the world, offering a way for people to become involved in local community hands-on initiatives in the light of peak oil and climate change. "Heart and Soul" groups emerged within this movement, initiated by Hilary Prentice (2012) and Sophy Banks, who later developed Inner Transition (2012). These groups work with the psychological, spiritual, and consciousness aspects of the transition to a sustainable human presence on the earth. This grassroots community movement for social and environmental change has thus brought together outer and inner change within the one movement, asking what does a healthy culture look like?

Psychotherapist Rosemary Randall and engineer Andy Brown started the psychosocial project Carbon Conversations in Cambridge, UK in 2006. This addressed the practicalities of carbon reduction while taking account of the complex emotions and social pressures that make living sustainably difficult.

WILDERNESS IMMERSION AND SOCIAL CHANGE

The Natural Change Project is an interesting mix of personal and social change, integrating psychotherapeutic knowledge, wilderness practice, and the change inspired by immersion in wilderness and group work in the form of a six-month course. This was initially facilitated by Dave Key and Margaret Kerr and funded by World Wildlife Fund (WWF) Scotland. They selected community leaders from the health, education, private, youth, arts, and NGO sectors in Scotland. None of the participants were previously active in the field of sustainability; one woman said at the start, "I thought nature was the gap between Harvey Nichols and the taxi door" (MacDonald, 2009). The project led to a range of outcomes at personal, organisational, and social levels. It created a group of high-profile leaders who became advocates for WWF's work in Scotland and beyond. This ultimately influenced government education policy and led to the recognition of Scotland by UNESCO as a world leader in Learning for Sustainability (Kerr & Key, 2012b). This project raises interesting questions about what inspires people to change their attitudes and relationship towards the earth.

THE POWER OF THE IMAGINATION

Using story and the imagination has been at the core of the Transition movement, founded by Rob Hopkins. He feels strongly that people need more than alarming facts to inspire them to action. Rather, the Transition movement has engaged people by imagining a green future that improves our lives, based on the ideas of permaculture (Hopkins, 2008). Allied to this is the movement of regenerative culture (Wahl, 2016) and re-wilding (Tree, 2018) which show how quickly the land as well as community can regenerate given the right support. These movements counter the commonly held beliefs that associate a green life with deprivation. They are based on finding a new story which is about living with nature, countering the old paradigm notion of fighting against nature.

THE ISSUE OF "POSITIVITY"

There is no doubt that positive visions and alternative stories of the future can inspire change. In fact, we desperately need to hear the many positive stories of change to counter the media's addiction to sensational bad news and to enable people to feel part of a worldwide community of change (Hawken, 2007). But many rightly say that positivity on its own is not enough. We need to understand the strength of the resistance to change, such as climate change denial, the dangers of misinformation deliberately being fed to the public by those with vested interests in the fossil fuel industries in order to create confusion and the threats to the lives of environmental activists and those reporting on corporate corruption (Hamilton, 2010). Extinction Rebellion and the youth climate strikes are part of a growing grassroots resistance movement who join many others who have been rising up for decades, such as Indigenous Rising, saying a powerful NO to business as usual. There are parallels, here, with the anti-smoking campaign and the misinformation spread by the tobacco industry, although obviously the global crisis we now face is on an altogether different scale.

There is a tendency for positivity and despair to become polarised, yet they are both a necessary part of a process. When grief and despair are actively listened to they usually pass of their own accord, like the waves of our inner emotional sea, giving way to renewal and resilience. Many fear getting stuck in these dark places and perhaps it is this fear which leads to trying to cheer up the grief-stricken friend or giving reasons to be positive.

We also know how hard it is to change the habits of a lifetime. We may try to be "positive" but end up doing things that we know are not good for ourselves, others, or the earth. Psychotherapy explores the unconscious wishes behind these actions, such as patterns of familiarity, the threat to a deeper sense of identity, the enjoyment or excitement of doing what is not allowed, the addiction to the quick fix or the refusal to give them up unless others do – such as flying to exotic places on holiday. Some people feel so enraged by the actions of humans they believe we do not deserve to be on this earth. This can lead to an unconscious wish for apocalypse, as if total wipe-out were easier than the struggle to hold the tension of opposites. Many rightly say that the concentration on personal change is misleading: we must have policy change. But let us not forget the many examples where policy change is consumer led, a reminder that personal and political cannot be split.

COMPASSION

Many in the green movement have been accused of being hypocritical for supporting green ideas while at the same time doing things which damage the ecosystem. Yet even when we try our best we inevitably contribute to the problem if we live within industrial growth culture. This can lead to a sense of nagging guilt, a sense of not living according to one's own values. Guilt can be double edged: it can push us into deeper enquiry and further action for the benefit of all beings but it can also lead to a fruitless self-flagellation. Compassion for self and others, as we struggle to do our best in difficult times, is vital. Active listening to where the other person is coming from helps develop compassion. Many are struggling to stay afloat in this society; many suffer from increasing trauma, overloaded and overwhelmed, bombarded with information, without the time to research what is truth and what is lies. There is an increasingly sophisticated fake news culture appearing. Choices arise out of this complex mix. Building community, solidarity with all our relations, is at the heart of recovery and this is surely founded on developing compassion.

THE QUESTION OF HOPE IN THE MIDST OF BLEAK TIMES

The question arising from many people's hearts right now is where do we find hope when the future looks so bleak? As the crisis quickens, and people start to face into and really feel what is happening, it is easy to fall into despair. Many people suspect there is little hope of averting climate change: the best we can do is adapt to the changes and mitigate the worst, preparing for system collapse in the coming decades. This is the conclusion of sustainability consultant Jem Bendall, whose recent paper "Deep Adaptation" (2018) has gone viral. His readers are at once relieved that he is unafraid of naming what they see as the reality of our situation, while at the same time many accuse him of spreading hopelessness.

Tolerating radical uncertainty is challenging, but this is a practice which offers a path beyond the game of hope and hopelessness, for uncertainty has the potential to bring us into the present moment, attuning ourselves to the energetic field of the other. That is where our strength lies. As T. S. Eliot wrote, "I said to my soul, be still and wait without hope, for hope would be hope for the wrong thing" (1940, p. 28).

"In the Navajo system most 'illness' [in the widest possible sense] results from some kind of disturbance of the natural balance in the cosmos. Much of Navajo etiology is based on a wound to/from nature" (Bernstein, 2005, p. 127). Applying this principle to our collective ills, it is possible to understand our environmental crisis, and climate change, as a wound that Western culture has inflicted on Nature. Our task, now, is to restore balance in ourselves and in the collective: this means paying attention to both individual and collective action. This is where I place my hope: that whatever the future outcome, whether we find renewal of life on earth or whether humans and many others of our relatives become extinct before the end of the century, we can still work towards restoring balance as far as possible. Repairing our relationship with others is always worth attending to, right to the end.

I find this is helpful in facing our situation. I have faith that the earth is powerful enough to rebalance herself in some way which may or may not include humans. Our task is to attend to the present moment. Beyond the countless practical tasks there is much to be done: a confusing mix of attending to the devastating losses as well as to the birthing of a new way of being in the world. In this liminal space, between old and new, there is great upheaval and our familiar containers are falling apart. People are anxious, despairing, and in a state of great tenderness as the skin of our culture is sloughing off. We are in need of a new form of cultural psychotherapy that helps us through this mother of all rites of passage.

I also cannot deny there are things I hope for. My greatest hope is that we do not walk into the fires and the floods asleep. That as many people as possible are able to wake up and attend to the crisis at hand. That we can work together and support each other on this tumultuous journey we are on. That we can be tender with one another as the situation worsens. That we can keep returning to the present, over and over again, offering gratitude to the earth, over and over again, for all that we are given. Then maybe, just maybe, there is a chance of a way through that lies beyond our current ways of understanding the world. For me this is keeping faith rather than holding onto hope and leaving the door open to miracles.

REFERENCES

Abram, D. (1997). *The Spell of the Sensuous: Perception and Language in a More-than-human World*. New York: Vintage.

Albrecht, G. (2007). Solastalgia: the distress caused by environmental change. *Australasian Psychiatry*, 15: 95–98.

Anthony, C. (1995). Ecopsychology and the deconstruction of whiteness. In: T. Roszak, A. Kanner, & M. Gomes (Eds.), *Ecopsychology: Restoring the Earth, Healing the Mind* (pp. 263–278). San Francisco, CA: Sierra Club.

Armstrong, J. (1995). The keepers of the Earth. In: T. Roszak, A. Kanner, & M. Gomes (Eds.), *Ecopsychology: Restoring the Earth, Healing the Mind* (pp. 316–324). San Francisco, CA: Sierra Club.

Arnstein, S. R. (1969). A ladder of citizen participation. *Journal of the American Planning Association*, 35(4): 216–224.

Banks, S. (2012). The Transition movement: inner and outer. An Interview by Ian McNay. https://youtube.com/watch?v=NJb-WfoE4Qoo (last accessed 31 December 2019).

Baring, A., & Cashford, J. (1991). *The Myth of the Goddess: Evolution of an Image*. London: Penguin.

Bates, B. (1983). *The Way of Wyrd*. London: Hay House.

Bateson, G. (1972). *Steps to an Ecology of Mind*. Chicago, IL: University of Chicago Press.

Bendall, J. (2018). Deep adaptation: A map for navigating climate tragedy. Occasional Paper 2. Institute of Leadership and Sustainability (IFLAS), University of Cumbria. www.iflas.info.

Berger, R. (2006). Beyond words: Nature therapy in action. *Journal of Critical Psychology, Counseling and Psychotherapy*, 6(4): 195–199.

Bernstein, J. (2005). *Living in the Borderland: The Evolution of Consciousness and the Challenge of Healing Trauma*. Hove, UK: Routledge.

Berry, T. (1978). The new story: Comments on the origin, identification and transmission of values. *Teilhard Studies*, 1 (Winter): 77–88.

Berry, T. (2006). *Evening Thoughts: Reflecting on Earth as Sacred Community*. San Francisco, CA: Sierra Club.

Birkeland, I., & Aasen, A. (2012). Ecopsychology and education: place literacy in early childhood education. In: M. J. Rust & N. Totton (Eds.), *Vital Signs: Psychological Responses to Ecological Crisis* (pp. 105–118). London: Karnac.

Blackie, S. (2016). *If Women Rose Rooted*. London: September.

Bodnar, S. (2008). Wasted and bombed: clinical enactments of a changing relationship to the Earth. *Psychoanalytic Dialogues*, 18(4): 484–512.

Brazier, C. (2018). *Ecotherapy in Practice: A Buddhist Model*. New York: Routledge.

Breytenbach, A. (2012). The Animal Communicator. Documentary film, Natural History Unit (NHU), Africa.

Buhner, S. H. (2004). *The Secret Teachings of Plants*. Rochester, VT: Bear.

Buzzell, L., & Edwards, S. (2009). The waking up syndrome. In: L. Buzzell & C. Chalquist, *Ecotherapy: Healing with Nature in Mind* (pp. 123–130). San Francisco, CA: Sierra Club.

Carson, R. (1962). *Silent Spring*. Boston, MA: Houghton Mifflin.

Chalquist, C. (2007). *Terrapsychology: Re-engaging the Soul of Place*. New Orleans, LA: Spring Journal.

Cole, B. (2019). Woman sets charred remains of her house destroyed by fire in front of Australian parliament. *Newsweek*. 2 December. https://newsweek.com/australia-bush-fires-scott-morrison-climate-change-melinda-plesman-1475016 (last accessed 15 December 2019).

Cooper Marcus, C., & Barnes, M. (1998). *Healing Gardens; Therapeutic Benefits and Design Recommendations*. Hoboken, NJ: John Wiley and Sons.

Coren, S., & Walker, J. (1997). *What Do Dogs Know?* New York: Simon & Schuster.

References

Deloria, V. (2009). *C. G. Jung and the Sioux Traditions: Dreams, Visions, Nature and the Primitive*. New Orleans, LA: Spring Journal.

Detweiler, M., Sharma, T., Detweiler, J., Murphy, P., Lane, S., Carmen, J., Chudhary, A., Halling, M., & Kim, K. (2012). What is the evidence to support the use of therapeutic gardens for the elderly? *Psychiatry Investigation*, 9(2): 100–110.

Dodds, J. (2011). *Psychoanalysis and Ecology at the Edge of Chaos*. London: Routledge.

Doherty, T. (2016). Theoretical and empirical foundations for ecotherapy. In: M. Jordan & J. Hinds (Eds.), *Ecotherapy: Research, Theory and Practice*. London: Palgrave.

Dunann Winter, D. (1996). *Ecological Psychology: Healing the Split between Planet and Self*. New York: Harper Collins.

Eisenstein, C. (2018). *Climate: A New Story*. Berkeley, CA: North Atlantic.

Eliot, T. S. (1940). Four Quartets, East Coker, Part 3. London: Faber & Faber.

Eyers, P. (2016). *Ancient Spirit Rising: Reclaiming Your Roots & Restoring Earth Community*. Otonabee, Ontario, Canada: Stone Circle Press.

Fisher, A. (2013). Ecopsychology at the crossroads: contesting the nature of a field. *Ecopsychology*, 5(3): 167–176.

Foster, S., & Little, M. (1989). *The Book of the Vision Quest: Personal Transformation in the Wilderness*. New York: Touchstone.

Fox, W. (1990). *Towards a Transpersonal Ecology: Developing New Foundations for Environmentalism*. Boston, MA: Shambhala.

Freud, S. (1930). *Civilisation and Its Discontents*. J. Strachey (Trans.). New York: W. W. Norton, 1961.

Fromm, E. (1973). *The Anatomy of Destructiveness*. New York: Holt, Rinehart & Winston.

Glendinning, C. (1994). *My Name is Chellis and I'm in Recovery from Western Civilisation*. Boston, MA: Shambhala.

Glendinning, C. (1995). Technology, trauma and the wild. In: T. Roszak, A. Kanner, & M. Gomes (Eds.), *Ecopsychology: Restoring the Earth, Healing the Mind* (pp. 41–54). San Francisco, CA: Sierra Club.

References

Gomes, M. (2009). Altars of extinction. In: L. Buzzell & C. Chalquist, *Ecotherapy: Healing with Nature in Mind* (pp. 246–250). San Francisco, CA: Sierra Club.

Greenway, R. (1995). The wilderness effect and ecopsychology. In: T. Roszak, A. Kanner, & M. Gomes (Eds.), *Ecopsychology: Restoring the Earth, Healing the Mind* (pp. 122–135). San Francisco, CA: Sierra Club.

Greenway, R. (2009). Robert Greenway: the Ecopsychology interview. *Ecopsychology*, 1(1): 47–52.

Griffin, S. (1979). *Woman and Nature: The Roaring Inside Her*. New York: Harper & Row.

Hall, K. (2012a). Remembering the forgotten tongue. In: M.-J. Rust & N. Totton (Eds.), *Vital Signs: Psychological Responses to Ecological Crisis* (pp. 79–88). London: Karnac.

Hall, K. (2012b). Equine Assisted Process. www.kelvinhall.info/ equine-assisted-process/4566953445 (last accessed 31 December 2019).

Hamilton, C. (2010). *Requiem for a Species*. New York: Earthscan.

Hawken, P. (2007). *Blessed Unrest: How the Largest Movement in the World Came into Being, and Why No One Saw It Coming*. New York: Penguin.

Hickman, C. (2019). Children and climate change: exploring children's feelings about climate change using free association narrative interview methodology. In: P. Hoggett (Ed.), *Climate Psychology: On Indifference to Disaster*. Cham, Switzerland: Palgrave Macmillan.

Hopkins, R. (2008). *The Transition Handbook: From Oil Dependency to Local Resilience*. Dartington, UK: Green Books.

Isaacson, R. (2009). *The Horse Boy: A Father's Miraculous Journey to Heal His Son*. London: Viking.

Jordan, M. (2005). The Vision Quest: A Transpersonal Process. Paper presented to the British Psychological Society, Transpersonal Psychology Section, 17th Conference.

Jordan, M. (2009). Nature and self: an ambivalent attachment. *Ecopsychology*, 1(1): 26–31.

References

Jordan, M. (2014). *Nature and Therapy: Understanding Psychotherapy and Counselling in Outdoor Spaces*. London: Routledge.

Jung, C. G. (1955). *Synchronicity: An Acausal Connecting Principle*. CW8. London: Routledge.

Jung, C. G. (1961). *Memories, Dreams, Reflections*. New York: Random House.

Jung, C. G. (1977). *The Symbolic Life: Miscellaneous Writings*. CW18. London: Routledge.

Kamalamani (2016). *Other than Mother – Choosing Childlessness with Life in Mind: A Private Decision with Global Consequences*. Alresford, UK: Earth Books.

Kerr, M., & Key, D. (2012a). The ecology of the unconscious. In: M.-J. Rust & N. Totton (Eds.), *Vital Signs: Psychological Responses to Ecological Crisis* (pp. 63–78). London: Karnac.

Kerr, M., & Key, D. (2012b). The Natural Change Project. In: M.-J. Rust & N. Totton (Eds.), *Vital Signs: Psychological Responses to Ecological Crisis* (pp. 239–252). London: Karnac.

Key, D. (2003). The Ecology of Adventure. Master of science thesis, Edinburgh: The Centre for Human Ecology. https://ecoself.net/resources/ (last accessed 31 December 2019).

Kidner, D. (2001). *Nature and Psyche: Radical Environmentalism and the Politics of Subjectivity*. Albany, NY: State University of New York Press.

LaChance, A. (1991). *Greenspirit: Twelve Steps in Ecological Spirituality. Shaftesbury*, UK: Element.

LaChapelle, D. (1992). *Sacred Land, Sacred Sex; Rapture of the Deep: Concerning Deep Ecology and Celebrating Life*. Skyland, NC: Kivaki.

Leopold, A. (1949). The land ethic. In: *A Sand County Almanac.* New York: Oxford University Press.

Lertzman, R. (2015). *Environmental Melancholia*. New York: Routledge.

Linden, S., & Grut, J. (2002). *The Healing Fields*. London: Frances Lincoln.

Louv, R. (2005). *Last Child in the Woods: Saving our Children from Nature-Deficit Disorder*. Chapel Hill, NC: Algonquin.

Mabey, R. (2007). *Naturecure*. Charlottesville, VA: University of Virginia Press.

Mabey, R. (2012). Interview, *All in the Mind*. BBC Sounds. www.bbc.co.uk/programmes/b01k1nl3 (last accessed 15 September 2019).

Macdonald, L.M. (2009). Changes and Gifts: taking stock. Blog article from the WWF Natural Change Project, posted 3 February, 2009. Currently archived offline. Edinburgh, UK: Natural Change Foundation.

Macfarlane, R. (2015). *Landmarks*. London: Hamish Hamilton.

Macy, J. (1990). The greening of the self. In: A. Badiner (Ed.), *Dharma Gaia: A Harvest of Essays in Buddhism and Ecology*. Berkeley, CA: Parallax.

Macy, J., & Johnstone, C. (2012). *Active Hope: How to Face the Mess We're in Without Going Crazy*. Novato, CA: New World Library.

Macy, J., & Young Brown, M. (1998). *Coming Back to Life: Practices to Reconnect Our Lives, Our World*. Gabriola Island, BC, Canada: New Society.

Main, R. (2007). *Revelations of Chance: Synchronicity as Spiritual Experience*. Albany, NY: State University of New York Press.

Maiteny, P. (2012). Longing to be human: evolving ourselves in healing the earth. In: M. J. Rust & N. Totton (Eds.), *Vital Signs: Psychological Responses to Ecological Crisis* (pp. 47–62). London: Karnac.

McIntosh, A. (2008). *Hell and High Water: Climate Change, Hope and the Human Condition*. Edinburgh, UK: Birlin.

Merchant, C. (1983). *The Death of Nature: Women, Ecology and the Scientific Revolution*. New York: Harper & Row.

MIND (2007). Report on Ecotherapy – the Green Agenda for Mental Health. www.mind.org.uk/media/273470/ecotherapy.pdf (last accessed 31 December 2019).

Naess, A. (1973). The shallow and the deep, long-range ecology movement: a summary. *Inquiry*, 16: 95–100.

Naess, A. (1988). Self-realisation: an ecological approach to being in the world. In: J. Seed, J. Macy, P. Fleming, & A. Naess (Eds.), *Thinking Like a Mountain: Towards a Council of All Beings*. Gabriola Island, BC, Canada: New Society.

References

Norberg-Hodge, H. (1992). *Ancient Futures: Learning from Ladakh*. San Francisco, CA: Sierra Club.

Peters, R. (1987). The eagle and the serpent: the minding of matter. *Journal of Analytical Psychology*, 32: 359–381.

Pinnock, D., & Douglas-Hamilton, D. (1997). *Gangs, Rituals and Rites of Passage*. Cape Town: African Sun.

Plotkin, B. (2003). *Soulcraft: Crossing into the Mysteries of Psyche and Nature*. Novato, CA: New World Library.

Plumwood, V. (1992). *Feminism and the Mastery of Nature*. London: Routledge.

Power, L. (2012). For kin and country. *Sydney Morning Herald*, 14 July.

Prechtel, M. (2009). *Secrets of the Talking Jaguar*. New York: Tarcher Putnam.

Prentice, H. (2001). The Sustainable Psyche – A Psychotherapist Introduces Ecopsychology. Keynote speech for Community Psychology, Race and Culture Special Interest Group Joint Annual Conference. http://hilaryprenticepsychotherapy.net/ecopsychology.htm (last accessed 31 December 2019).

Prentice, H. (2003). The cosmic spiral. *Psychotherapy and Politics International*, 1(1): 32–46.

Prentice, H. (2012). "Heart and soul": inner and outer within the Transition Movement. In: M. J. Rust & N. Totton (Eds.), *Vital Signs: Psychological Responses to Ecological Crisis* (pp. 175–190). London: Karnac.

Randall, R. (2009). Loss and climate change: the cost of parallel narratives. *Ecopsychology*, 1(3): 118–129.

Robertson, C. (2016). Cultural Repair. https://culture-crisis.net/blog-cultural-repair.html (last accessed 31 December 2019).

Romanyshyn, R. (2011). Metabletics: Foundation for a Therapy of Culture. http://robertromanyshyn.jigsy.com/articles (last accessed 31 December 2019).

Roszak, T. (1992). *The Voice of the Earth*. New York: Simon & Schuster.

Roszak, T., Kanner, A., & Gomes, M. (Eds.) (1995). *Ecopsychology: Restoring the Earth, Healing the Mind*. San Francisco, CA: Sierra Club.

Rubin, C. (2019). Oliver Sacks: The Healing Power of Gardens.

New York Times, 18 April. www.nytimes.com/2019/04/18/opinion/sunday/oliver-sacks-gardens.html (last accessed 31 December 2019).

Rust, M.-J. (2005). Ecolimia nervosa? *Therapy Today*, 16(10): 11–15.

Rust, M.-J. (2008a). Climate on the couch: unconscious processes in relation to our environmental crisis. *Psychotherapy and Politics International*, 6(3): 157–170.

Rust, M.-J. (2008b). Nature hunger. *Counselling Psychology Review*, 23: 2.

Rust, M.-J. (2009). Nature as subject: exploring anthropocentrism. *British Holistic Medical Association Journal*, 6(3): 31–35.

Rust, M.-J. (2011). Shadow and Transformation. Schumacher College, video lecture. https://schumachercollege.org.uk/resources/audio-video-archive (last accessed 31 December 2019).

Rust, M.-J. (2014). Eros, animal and Earth. *Self and Society, International Journal for Humanistic Psychology*, 41(4): 38–43.

Ryde, J. (2010). Dog-walking: not just a walk in the park. Reflections on relationships with dogs and inner landscapes. In: Bennett, P., Montreal 2010. *Facing Multiplicity: Psyche, Nature, Culture. Proceedings of the XV111th Congress of the International Association of Analytical Psychology* (pp. 477–486). Einsiedeln, Switzerland: Daimon Verlag.

Samuels, A. (1993). *The Political Psyche*. London: Routledge.

Searles, H. (1960). *The Non-Human Environment in Normal Development and in Schizophrenia*. New York: International Universities Press.

Seed, J. (1988). Beyond anthropocentrism. In: J. Seed, J. Macy, P. Fleming, & A. Naess (Eds.), *Thinking Like a Mountain: Towards a Council of All Beings* (pp. 35–40). Gabriola Island, BC, Canada: New Society.

Sessions, G. (1995). *Deep Ecology for the 21st Century*. Boston, MA: Shambhala.

Sheldrake, R. (1990). *The Rebirth of Nature: The Greening of Science and God*. London: Rider.

References

Shepard, P. (1982). *Nature and Madness*. San Francisco, CA: Sierra Club.

Siddons Heginworth, I. (2008). *Environmental Arts Therapy and the Tree of Life*. Exeter, UK: Spirit's Rest.

Singer, T. (2018). Extinction anxiety and Donald Trump: where the spirit of the depths meets the spirit of the times. In: J. Gartner, S. Buser, & L. Cruz (Eds.), *Rocket Man: Nuclear Madness and the Mind of Donald Trump* (pp. 205–213). Asheville, NC: Chiron.

Somé, M. (1995). *Of Water and the Spirit: Ritual, Magic and Initiation in the Life of an African Shaman*. New York: Penguin Arkana.

Tacey, D. (2009). *Edge of the Sacred: Jung, Psyche, Earth*. Einsiedeln, Switzerland: Daimon Verlag.

Tarnas, R. (2007). *Cosmos and Psyche*. New York: Penguin.

Totton, N. (2011). *Wild Therapy: Undomesticating Inner and Outer Worlds*. Ross-on-Wye, UK: PCCS Books.

Totton, N. (2016). Let the right one in: talking about climate change in therapy. *The Psychotherapist*, UKCP Magazine, 63: 15–16.

Tree, I. (2018). *Wilding: The Return of Nature to a British Farm*. London: Picador.

Wahl, D. (2016). *Designing Regenerative Cultures*. Axminster, UK: Triarchy Press.

Waldo Emerson, R. (1844). The poet. In: J. Slater, A. R. Ferguson & J. F. Carr (Eds.), *The Collected Works of Ralph Waldo Emerson, Vol. III, Essays*, second series. Cambridge, MA: Harvard University Press.

Wall Kimmerer, R. (2013). *Braiding Sweetgrass: Indigenous Wisdom, Scientific Knowledge and the Teachings of Plants*. Minneapolis, MN: Milkweed Editions.

Weintrobe, S. (2012). The difficult problem of anxiety when thinking about climate change. In: S. Weintrobe (Ed.), *Engaging with Climate Change* (pp. 33–47). London: Routledge.

Weintrobe, S. (2013). *Response to Polly Higgins: "The Earth Needs a Good Lawyer"* . Climate Psychology Alliance Conference, "Psyche, Law and Justice", London.

Weller, F. (2015). *The Wild Edge of Sorrow: Rituals of Renewal and the Sacred Work of Grief.* Berkeley, CA: North Atlantic.

Wilson, E. O. (1984). *The Biophilia Hypothesis.* Covelo, CA: Shearwater.

Woodbury, Z. (2019). Climate trauma: toward a new taxonomy of trauma. *Ecopsychology*, 11(1): 1–8.

INDEX

Index

Index

Index

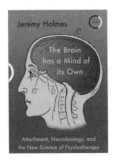

Body Psychotherapy for the 21st Century
Nick Totton

Body psychotherapy currently attracts more interest than ever before, bringing awareness of embodiment into what has been a verbally oriented profession. The approach has developed to engage with other fields including neuroscience, phenomenology, and cognitive studies, as well as the relational turn in psychotherapy. Using a historical survey to chart this transformation, the author shows how four distinct versions of embodied practice have interacted to generate the current field.

ISBN 978-1-913494-04-9 (pbk)   ISBN 978-1-913494-05-6 (e-book)   168 Pages   £12.99

Pathologies of the Self
Exploring Narcissistic and Borderline States of Mind
Phil Mollon

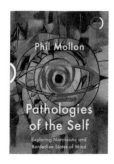

Collectively, we are trapped in images of self, whether constructed by us, or imposed by others. These illusions are inextricably bound to our sense of who we are, and sometimes defended so fiercely that it leads to narcissistic disturbances and borderline states of mind. In this fascinating book Phil Mollon explores narcissistic phenomena in both the clinic and everyday life, demonstrating the illusory nature of the self, and showing how, beneath our defences, we are all 'borderline'.

ISBN 978-1-913494-00-1 (pbk)   ISBN 978-1-913494-01-8 (e-book)   176 Pages   £12.99

www.confer.uk.com

The New Sexual Landscape and Contemporary Psychoanalysis

Danielle Knafo and Rocco Lo Bosco

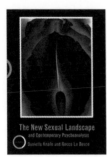

The New Sexual Landscape
and Contemporary Psychoanalysis
Danielle Knafo and Rocco Lo Bosco

The sexual landscape has changed dramatically in the past few decades, with the meaning of gender and sexuality now being parsed within the realms of gender fluidity, nonheteronormative sexuality, BDSM, and polyamory. The sea change in sexual attitudes has also made room for the mainstreaming of internet pornography and the use of virtual reality for sexual pleasure – and the tech gurus have not even scratched the surface when it comes to mining the possibilities of alternative realities. *The New Sexual Landscape and Contemporary Psychoanalysis* surveys modern sex culture and suggests ways psychoanalysis can update its theories and practice to meet the novel needs of today's generations.

ISBN 978-1-913494-18-6 (pbk)   ISBN ISBN 978-1-913494-19-3 (e-book)   216 Pages   £12.99